The Constitution of the
State of Kentucky:
A Quick Reference Guide

Bootblack Budget Books
Copyright 2018 ©
ISBN-13: 978-1986177511
ISBN-10: 1986177513

Contents:

Preamble – Page 24

Bill of Rights – Page 25

Section 1. Rights of life, liberty, worship, pursuit of safety and happiness, free speech, acquiring and protecting property, peaceable assembly, redress of grievances, bearing arms.

Section 2. Absolute and arbitrary power denied.

Section 3. Men are equal -- No exclusive grant except for public services -- Property not to be exempted from taxation -- Grants revocable.

Section 4. Power inherent in the people -- Right to alter, reform, or abolish government.

Section 5. Right of religious freedom.

Section 6. Elections to be free and equal.

Section 7. Right of trial by jury.

Section 8. Freedom of speech and of the press.

Section 9. Truth may be given in evidence in prosecution for publishing matters proper for public information -- Jury to try law and facts in libel prosecutions.

Section 10. Security from search and seizure -- Conditions of issuance of warrant.

Section 11. Rights of accused in criminal prosecution -- Change of venue.

Section 12. Indictable offense not to be prosecuted by information -- Exceptions.

Section 13. Double jeopardy -- Property not to be taken for public use without compensation.

Section 14. Right of judicial remedy for injury -- Speedy trial.

Section 15. Laws to be suspended only by General Assembly.

Section 16. Right to bail -- Habeas corpus.

Section 17. Excessive bail or fine, or cruel punishment, prohibited.

Section 18. Imprisonment for debt restricted.

Section 19. Ex post facto law or law impairing contract forbidden -- Rules of construction for mineral deeds relating to coal extraction.

Section 20. Attainder, operation of restricted.

Section 21. Descent in case of suicide or casualty.

Section 22. Standing armies restricted -- Military subordinate to civil -- Quartering soldiers restricted.

Section 23. No office of nobility or hereditary distinction, or for longer than a term of years.

Section 24. Emigration to be free.

Section 25. Slavery and involuntary servitude forbidden.

Section 26. General powers subordinate to Bill of Rights -- Laws contrary thereto are void.

Distribution of the Powers of Government - Page 31

Section 27. Powers of government divided among legislative, executive, and judicial departments.

Section 28. One department not to exercise power belonging to another.

The Legislative Department - Page 32

Section 29. Legislative power vested in General Assembly.

Section 30. Term of office of Senators and Representatives.

Section 31. Time of election and term of office of Senators and Representatives.

Section 32. Qualifications of Senators and Representatives.

Section 33. Senatorial and Representative districts.

Section 34. Officers of Houses of General Assembly.

Section 35. Number of Senators and Representatives.

Section 36. Time and place of meetings of General Assembly.

Section 37. Majority constitutes quorum -- Powers of less than a quorum.

Section 38. Each House to judge qualifications, elections, and returns of its members -- Contests.

Section 39. Powers of each House as to rules and conduct of members -- Contempt -- Bribery.

Section 40. Journals -- When vote to be entered.

Section 41. Adjournment during session.

Section 42. Compensation of members -- Length of sessions -- Legislative day.

Section 43. Privileges from arrest and from questioning as to speech or debate.

Section 44. Ineligibility of members to civil office created or given increased compensation during term.

Section 45. Collector of public money ineligible unless he has quietus.

Section 46. Bills must be reported by committee, printed, and read -- How bill called from committee -- Votes required for passage.

Section 47. Bills to raise revenue must originate in House of Representatives.

Section 48. Resources of Sinking Fund not to be diminished -- Preservation of fund.

Section 49. Power to contract debts -- Limit.

Section 50. Purposes for which debt may be contracted -- Tax to discharge -- Public vote.

Section 51. Law may not relate to more than one subject, to be expressed in title -- Amendments must be at length.

Section 52. General Assembly may not release debt to State or to county or city.

Section 53. Investigation of accounts of Treasurer and Auditor -- Report, publication, submission to Governor and General Assembly.

Section 54. No restriction on recovery for injury or death.

Section 55. When laws to take effect -- Emergency legislation.

Section 56. Signing of bills -- Enrollment -- Presentation to Governor.

Section 57. Member having personal interest to make disclosure and not vote.

Section 58. General Assembly not to audit nor allow private claim -- Exception -- Appropriations.

Section 59. Local and special legislation.

Section 60. General law not to be made special or local by amendment -- No special powers or privileges -- Law not to take effect on approval of other authority than General Assembly -- Exceptions.

Section 61. Provision to be made for local option on sale of liquor -- Time of elections.

Section 62. Style of laws.

Counties and County Seats - Page 44

Section 63. Area of counties -- Boundaries -- Creation and abolishment of counties.

Section 64. Division of county or removal of county seat, election required -- Minimum population of county.

Section 65. Striking territory from county -- Liability for indebtedness.

Impeachments - Page 45

Section 66. Power of impeachment vested in House.

Section 67. Trial of impeachments by Senate.

Section 68. Civil officers liable to impeachment -- Judgment -- Criminal liability.

The Executive Department:

Officers for the State at Large – Page 46

Section 69. Executive power vested in Governor.

Section 70. Election of Governor and Lieutenant Governor -- Term -- Tie vote.

Section 71. Gubernatorial succession.

Section 72. Qualifications of Governor and Lieutenant Governor -- Duties of Lieutenant Governor.

Section 73. When terms of Governor and Lieutenant Governor begin.

Section 74. Compensation of Governor and Lieutenant Governor.

Section 75. Governor is Commander-in-Chief of army, navy and militia.

Section 76. Power of Governor to fill vacancies.

Section 77. Power of Governor to remit fines and forfeitures, grant reprieves and pardons -- No power to remit fees.

Section 78. Governor may require information from state officers.

Section 79. Reports and recommendations to General Assembly.

Section 80. Governor may call extraordinary session of General Assembly, adjourn General Assembly.

Section 81. Governor to enforce laws.

Section 82. Succession of Lieutenant Governor.

Section 83. Repealed.

Section 84. When Lieutenant Governor to act as Governor -- President of the Senate not to preside at impeachment of Governor -- Certification of disability of Governor.

Section 85. President of Senate -- Election -- Powers.

Section 86. Compensation of President of the Senate.

Section 87. Who to act as Governor in absence of Lieutenant Governor and President of the Senate.

Section 88. Signature of bills by Governor -- Veto -- Passage over veto -- Partial veto.

Section 89. Concurrent orders and resolutions on same footing as bill.

Section 90. Contest of election for Governor or Lieutenant Governor.

Section 91. Constitutional State officers -- Election -- Qualifications -- Term of office -- Duties -- Secretary of State to record acts of Governor and report them to General Assembly.

Section 92. Qualifications of Attorney General.

Section 93. Succession of elected Constitutional State Officers -- Duties -- Inferior officers and members of boards and commissions.

Section 94. Repealed.

Section 95. Time of election of elected Constitutional State officers.

Section 96. Compensation of Constitutional State officers.

Officers for Districts and Counties – Page 53

Section 97. Commonwealth's Attorney and Circuit Court Clerk -- Election -- Term.

Section 98. Compensation of Commonwealth's Attorney.

Section 99. County officers, justices of the peace, and constables -- Election -- Term.

Section 100. Qualifications of officers for counties and districts.

Section 101. Qualifications and jurisdiction of constables.

Section 102. Officers for new counties.

Section 103. Bonds of county officers and other officers.

Section 104. Abolishment of office of assessor -- Assessor may not succeed himself.

Section 105. Consolidation of offices of sheriff and jailer.

Section 106. Fees of county officers -- Fees in counties having seventy-five thousand population or more.

Section 107. Additional county or district offices may be created.

Section 108. Abolishment of office of commonwealth's attorney.

The Judicial Department – Page 56

Section 109. The judicial power -- Unified system -- Impeachment.

The Supreme Court – Page 57

Section 110. Jurisdiction -- Quorum -- Special justices -- Districts -- Chief Justice.

The Court of Appeals – Page 59

Section 111. Composition -- Jurisdiction -- Administration -- Panels.

The Circuit Court – Page 60

Section 112. Location -- Circuits -- Composition -- Administration -- Jurisdiction.

The District Court – Page 61

Section 113. Location -- Districts -- Composition -- Administration -- Trial commissioners -- Jurisdiction.

Clerks of Courts - Page 63

Section 114. Selection -- Removal.

Appellate Policy-Rule-Making Power - Page 64

Section 115. Right of appeal -- Procedure.

Section 116. Rules governing jurisdiction, personnel, procedure, bar membership.

Offices of Justices and Judges - Page 65

Section 117. Election.

Section 118. Vacancies.

Section 119. Terms of office.

Section 120. Compensation -- Expenses.

Section 121. Retirement and removal.

Section 122. Eligibility.

Section 123. Prohibited activities.

Section 124. Conflicting provisions.

Section 125. Repealed

Section 126. Repealed

Section 127. Repealed

Section 128. Repealed

Section 129. Repealed

Section 130. Repealed

Section 131. Repealed

Section 132. Repealed

Section 133. Repealed

Section 134. Repealed

Section 135. Repealed

Section 136. Repealed

Section 137. Repealed

Section 138. Repealed

Section 139. Repealed

County Courts - Page 68

Section 140. County Court for each county -- Judge -- Compensation -- Commission -- Removal.

Section 141. Repealed.

Justices of the Peace - Page 69

Section 142. Justices' districts -- One Justice for each district -- Jurisdiction and powers of Justices -- Commissions -- Removal.

Section 143. Repealed.

Fiscal Courts - Page 70

Section 144. Fiscal Court for each county -- To consist of Justices of the Peace or Commissioners, and County Judge -- Quorum.

SUFFRAGE AND ELECTIONS – Page 71

Section 145. Persons entitled to vote.

Section 146. Soldiers or sailors stationed in State are not residents.

Section 147. Registration of voters -- Manner of voting -- Absent voting -- Voting machines -- "Election" defined -- Election laws -- Illiterate and disabled voters.

Section 148. Number of elections -- Day and hours of election -- Qualifications of officers -- Employees to be given time to vote.

Section 149. Privilege from arrest during voting.

Section 150. Disqualification from office for using money or property to secure or influence election -- Corporation not to use money or other thing of value to influence election -- Exclusion from office for conviction of felony or high misdemeanor - - Laws to regulate elections.

Section 151. Person guilty of fraud, intimidation, bribery, or corrupt practice to be deprived of office by suitable statutory means.

Section 152. Vacancies -- When filled by appointment, when by election-- Who to fill.

Section 153. Power of General Assembly as to elections.

Section 154. Laws as to sale or gift of liquor on election days.

Section 155. School elections not governed by Constitution.

MUNICIPALITIES – Page 75

Section 156. Repealed.

Section 156a. General Assembly authorized to provide for creation, governmental structure, and classification of cities.

Section 156b. General Assembly authorized to permit municipal home rule for cities.

Section 157. Maximum tax rate for cities, counties, and taxing districts.

Section 157a. Credit of Commonwealth may be loaned or given to county for roads -- County may vote to incur indebtedness and levy additional tax for roads.

Section 157b. Adoption of budget required for cities, counties, and taxing districts -- Expenditures not to exceed revenues for fiscal year.

Section 158. Maximum indebtedness of cities, counties, and taxing districts -- General Assembly authorized to set additional limits and conditions.

Section 159. Tax to pay indebtedness in not more than forty years must be levied.

Section 160. Municipal officers -- Election and term of office -- Officers ineligible -- Fiscal officers.

Section 161. Compensation of city, county, or municipal officer not to be changed after election or appointment or during term, nor term extended.

Section 162. Unauthorized contracts of cities, counties, and municipalities are void.

Section 163. Public utilities must obtain franchise to use streets.

Section 164. Term of franchises limited -- Advertisement and bids.

Section 165. Incompatible offices and employments.

Section 166. Expiration of city charters granted prior to Constitution.

Section 167. Time of election of city, urban-county, and town officers.

Section 168. Ordinance not to fix less penalty than statute for same offense -- Prosecution under one a bar.

REVENUE AND TAXATION – Page 81

Section 169. Fiscal year.

Section 170. Property exempt from taxation -- Cities may exempt factories for five years.

Section 171. State tax to be levied -- Taxes to be levied and collected for public purposes only and by general laws, and to be uniform within classes -- Classification of property for taxation -- Bonds exempt -- Referendum on act classifying property.

Section 172. Property to be assessed at fair cash value -- Punishment of assessor for willful error.

Section 172A. Assessment for ad valorem tax purposes of agricultural and horticultural land.

Section 172B. Property assessment or reassessment moratoriums.

Section 173. Officer receiving profit on public funds guilty of felony.

Section 174. Property to be taxed according to value, whether corporate or individual -- Income, license, and franchise taxes.

Section 175. Power to tax property not to be surrendered.

Section 176. Commonwealth not to assume debt of county or city -- Exception.

Section 177. Commonwealth not to lend credit, nor become stockholder in corporation, nor build railroad or highway.

Section 178. Law for borrowing money to specify purpose, for which alone money may be used.

Section 179. Political subdivision not to become stockholder in corporation, or appropriate money or lend credit to any person, except for roads or State Capitol.

Section 180. Act or ordinance levying any tax must specify purpose, for which alone money may be used.

Section 181. General Assembly may not levy tax for political subdivision, but may confer power - - License and excise taxes -- City taxes in lieu of ad valorem taxes.

Section 182. Railroad taxes -- How assessed and collected.

EDUCATION – Page 87

Section 183. General Assembly to provide for school system.

Section 184. Common school fund -- What constitutes -- Use -- Vote on tax for education other than in common schools.

Section 185. Interest on school fund -- Investment.

Section 186. Distribution and use of school fund.

Section 187. Race or color not to affect distribution of school fund.

Section 188. Refund of Federal direct tax part of school fund -- Irredeemable bond.

Section 189. School money not to be used for church, sectarian, or denominational school.

CORPORATIONS – Page 89

Section 190. Regulation of corporations by General Assembly.

Section 191. Repealed.

Section 192. Repealed.

Section 193. Repealed.

Section 194. Repealed.

Section 195. Corporation property subject to eminent domain -- Corporations not to infringe upon individuals.

Section 196. Regulation of common carriers -- No relief from common-law liability.

Section 197. Free passes or reduced rates to officers forbidden.

Section 198. Repealed.

Section 199. Telegraph and telephone companies -- Right to construct lines -- Exchange of messages.

Section 200. Repealed.

Section 201. Public utility company not to consolidate with, acquire or operate competing or parallel system -- Common carriers not to share earnings with one not carrying -- Telephone companies excepted under certain conditions.

Section 202. Repealed.

Section 203. Repealed.

Section 204. Bank officer liable for receiving deposit for insolvent bank.

Section 205. Forfeiture of corporate charters in case of abuse or detrimental use.

Section 206. Warehouses subject to legislative control -- Inspection -- Protection of patrons.

Section 207. Repealed.

Section 208. Repealed.

RAILROADS AND COMMERCE – Page 93

Section 209. Repealed.

Section 210. Common carrier corporation not to be interested in other business.

Section 211. Foreign railroad corporation may not condemn or acquire real estate.

Section 212. Rolling stock, earnings, and personal property of railroads subject to execution or attachment.

Section 213. Railroad companies to handle traffic with connecting carriers without discrimination.

Section 214. Railroad not to make exclusive or preferential contract.

Section 215. Freight to be handled without discrimination.

Section 216. Railroad must allow tracks of others to cross or unite.

Section 217. Penalties for violating Sections 213, 214, 215, or 216 -- Attorney General to enforce.

Section 218. Long and short hauls.

THE MILITIA – Page 97

Section 219. Militia, what to consist of.

Section 220. General Assembly to provide for militia -- Exemptions from service.

Section 221. Government of militia to conform to Army regulations.

Section 222. Officers of militia -- Adjutant General.

Section 223. Safekeeping of public arms, military records, relics, and banners.

GENERAL PROVISIONS – Page 99

Section 224. Bonds -- What officers to give -- Liability on.

Section 225. Armed men not to be brought into State -- Exception.

Section 226. State lottery -- Charitable lotteries and charitable gift enterprises -- Other lotteries and gift enterprises forbidden.

Section 226a. Repealed.

Section 227. Prosecution and removal of local officers for misfeasance, malfeasance, or neglect.

Section 228. Oath of officers and attorneys.

Section 229. "Treason" defined -- Evidence necessary to convict.

Section 230. Money not to be drawn from Treasury unless appropriated -- Annual publication of accounts -- Certain revenues usable only for highway purposes.

Section 231. Suits against the Commonwealth.

Section 232. Manner of administering oath.

Section 233. General laws of Virginia in force in this State until repealed.

Section 233A. Valid or recognized marriage -- Legal status of unmarried individuals.

Section 234. Residence and place of office of public officers.

Section 235. Salaries of public officers not to be changed during term -- Deductions for neglect.

Section 236. When officers to enter upon duties.

Section 237. Federal office incompatible with State office.

Section 238. Discharge of sureties on officers' bonds.

Section 239. Disqualification from office for presenting or accepting challenge to duel -- Further punishment.

Section 240. Pardon of person convicted of dueling.

Section 241. Recovery for wrongful death.

Section 242. Just compensation to be made in condemning private property -- Right of appeal -- Jury trial.

Section 243. Child labor.

Section 244. Wage-earners in industry or of corporations to be paid in money.

Section 244a. Old age assistance.

Section 245. Revision of statutes to conform to Constitution.

Section 246. Maximum limit on compensation of public officers.

Section 247. Public printing -- Contract for -- Officers not to have interest in -- Governor to approve.

Section 248. Juries -- Number of jurors -- Three-fourths may indict or give verdict.

Section 249. Employees of General Assembly -- Number and compensation.

Section 250. Arbitration, method for to be provided.

Section 251. Limitation of actions to recover possession of land based on early patents.

Section 252. Houses of reform to be established and maintained.

Section 253. Working of penitentiary prisoners -- When and where permitted.

Section 254. Control and support of convicts -- Leasing of labor.

Section 255. Frankfort is state capital.

Section 255A. Personal right to hunt, fish, and harvest wildlife - Limitations.

MODE OF REVISION – Page 110

Section 256. Amendments to Constitution -- How proposed and voted upon.

Section 257. Publication of proposed amendments.

Section 258. Constitutional Convention -- How proposed, voted upon, and called.

Section 259. Number and qualifications of delegates.

Section 260. Election of delegates -- meeting.

Section 261. Certification of election and compensation of delegates.

Section 262. Determination of election and qualifications of delegates -- Contests.

Section 263. Notice of election on question of calling convention.

Schedule and Ordinance – Page 113

Preamble:

We, the people of the Commonwealth of Kentucky, grateful to Almighty God for the civil, political and religious liberties we enjoy, and invoking the continuance of these blessings, do ordain and establish this Constitution.

BILL OF RIGHTS

That the great and essential principles of liberty and free government may be recognized and established, we declare that:

Section 1. All men are, by nature, free and equal, and have certain inherent and inalienable rights, among which may be reckoned:

First: The right of enjoying and defending their lives and liberties.

Second: The right of worshipping Almighty God according to the dictates of their consciences.

Third: The right of seeking and pursuing their safety and happiness.

Fourth: The right of freely communicating their thoughts and opinions.

Fifth: The right of acquiring and protecting property.

Sixth: The right of assembling together in a peaceable manner for their common good, and of applying to those invested with the power of government for redress of grievances or other proper purposes, by petition, address or remonstrance.

Seventh: The right to bear arms in defense of themselves and of the State, subject to the power of the General Assembly to enact laws to prevent persons from carrying concealed weapons.

Section 2. Absolute and arbitrary power over the lives, liberty and property of freemen exists nowhere in a republic, not even in the largest majority.

Section 3. All men, when they form a social compact, are equal; and no grant of exclusive, separate public emoluments or privileges shall be made to any man or set of men, except in consideration of public services; but no property shall be exempt from taxation except as provided in this Constitution, and every grant of a franchise, privilege or exemption, shall remain subject to revocation, alteration or amendment.

Section 4. All power is inherent in the people, and all free governments are founded on their authority and instituted for their peace, safety, happiness and the protection of property. For the advancement of these ends, they have at all times an inalienable and indefeasible right to alter, reform or abolish their government in such manner as they may deem proper.

Section 5. No preference shall ever be given by law to any religious sect, society or denomination; nor to any particular creed, mode of worship or system of ecclesiastical polity; nor shall any person be compelled to attend any place of worship, to contribute to the erection or maintenance of any such place, or to the salary or support of any minister of religion; nor shall any man be compelled to send his child to any school to which he may be conscientiously opposed; and the civil rights, privileges or capacities of no person shall be taken away, or in anywise diminished or enlarged, on account of his belief or disbelief of any religious tenet, dogma or teaching. No human authority shall, in any case whatever, control or interfere with the rights of conscience.

Section 6. All elections shall be free and equal.

Section 7. The ancient mode of trial by jury shall be held sacred, and the right thereof remain inviolate, subject to such modifications as may be authorized by this Constitution.

Section 8. Printing presses shall be free to every person who undertakes to examine the proceedings of the General Assembly or any branch of government, and no law shall ever be made to restrain the right thereof. Every person may freely and fully speak, write and print on any subject, being responsible for the abuse of that liberty.

Section 9. In prosecutions for the publication of papers investigating the official conduct of officers or men in a public capacity, or where the matter published is proper for public information, the truth thereof may be given in evidence; and in all indictments for libel the jury shall have the right to determine the law and the facts, under the direction of the court, as in other cases.

Section 10. The people shall be secure in their persons, houses, papers and possessions, from unreasonable search and seizure; and no warrant shall issue to search any place, or seize any person or thing, without describing them as nearly as may be, nor without probable cause supported by oath or affirmation.

Section 11. In all criminal prosecutions the accused has the right to be heard by himself and counsel; to demand the nature and cause of the accusation against him; to meet the witnesses face to face, and to have compulsory process for obtaining witnesses in his favor. He cannot be compelled to give evidence against himself, nor can he be deprived of his life, liberty or property, unless by the judgment of his peers or the law of the land; and in prosecutions by indictment or information, he shall have a speedy public trial by an impartial jury of the vicinage; but the General Assembly may provide by a general law for a change of venue in such prosecutions for both the defendant and the Commonwealth, the change to be made to the most convenient county in which a fair trial can be obtained.

Section 12. No person, for an indictable offense, shall be proceeded against criminally by information, except in cases arising in the land or naval forces, or in the militia, when in actual service, in time of war or public danger, or by leave of court for oppression or misdemeanor in office.

Section 13. No person shall, for the same offense, be twice put in jeopardy of his life or limb, nor shall any man's property be taken or applied to public use without the consent of his representatives, and without just compensation being previously made to him.

Section 14. All courts shall be open, and every person for an injury done him in his lands, goods, person or reputation, shall have remedy by due course of law, and right and justice administered without sale, denial or delay.

Section 15. No power to suspend laws shall be exercised unless by the General Assembly or its authority.

Section 16. All prisoners shall be bailable by sufficient securities, unless for capital offenses when the proof is evident or the presumption great: and the privilege of the writ of habeas corpus shall not be suspended unless when, in case of rebellion or invasion, the public safety may require it.

Section 17. Excessive bail shall not be required, nor excessive fines imposed, nor cruel punishment inflicted.

Section 18. The person of a debtor, where there is not strong presumption of fraud, shall not be continued in prison after delivering up his estate for the benefit of his creditors in such manner as shall be prescribed by law.

Section 19. (1) No ex post facto law, nor any law impairing the obligation of contracts, shall be enacted.

(2) In any instrument heretofore or hereafter executed purporting to sever the surface and mineral estates or to grant a mineral estate or to grant a right to extract minerals, which fails to state or describe in express and specific terms the method of coal extraction to be employed, or where said instrument contains language subordinating the surface estate to the mineral estate, it shall be held, in the absence of clear and convincing evidence to the contrary, that the intention of the parties to the instrument was that the coal be extracted only by the method or methods of commercial coal extraction commonly known to be in use in Kentucky in the area affected at the time the instrument was executed, and that the mineral estate be dominant to the surface estate for the purposes of coal extraction by only the method or methods of commercial coal extraction commonly known to be in use in Kentucky in the area affected at the time the instrument was executed.

Section 20. No person shall be attainted of treason or felony by the General Assembly, and no attainder shall work corruption of blood, nor, except during the life of the offender, forfeiture of estate to the Commonwealth.

Section 21. The estate of such persons as shall destroy their own lives shall descend or vest as in cases of natural death; and if any person shall be killed by casualty, there shall be no forfeiture by reason thereof.

Section 22. No standing army shall, in time of peace, be maintained without the consent of the General Assembly; and the military shall, in all cases and at all times, be in strict subordination to the civil power; nor shall any soldier, in time of peace, be quartered in any house without the consent of the owner, nor in time of war, except in a manner prescribed by law.

Section 23. The General Assembly shall not grant any title of nobility or hereditary distinction, nor create any office the appointment of which shall be for a longer time than a term of years.

Section 24. Emigration from the State shall not be prohibited.

Section 25. Slavery and involuntary servitude in this State are forbidden, except as a punishment for crime, whereof the party shall have been duly convicted.

Section 26. To guard against transgression of the high powers which we have delegated, We Declare that every thing in this Bill of Rights is excepted out of the general powers of government, and shall forever remain inviolate; and all laws contrary thereto, or contrary to this Constitution, shall be void.

Distribution of the Powers of Government

Section 27. The powers of the government of the Commonwealth of Kentucky shall be divided into three distinct departments, and each of them be confined to a separate body of magistracy, to wit: Those which are legislative, to one; those which are executive, to another; and those which are judicial, to another.

Section 28. No person or collection of persons, being of one of those departments, shall exercise any power properly belonging to either of the others, except in the instances hereinafter expressly directed or permitted.

The Legislative Department

Section 29. The legislative power shall be vested in a House of Representatives and a Senate, which, together, shall be styled the "General Assembly of the Commonwealth of Kentucky."

Section 30. Members of the House of Representatives and Senators shall be elected at the general election in even-numbered years for terms of four years for Senators and two years for members of the House of Representatives. The term of office of Representatives and Senators shall begin upon the first day of January of the year succeeding their election.

Section 31. At the general election to be held in November, 1984, and every two years thereafter, there shall be elected for four years one Senator in each Senatorial District in which the term of his predecessor in office will then expire and in every Representative District one Representative for two years.

Section 32. No person shall be a Representative who, at the time of his election, is not a citizen of Kentucky, has not attained the age of twenty-four years, and who has not resided in this State two years next preceding his election, and the last year thereof in the county, town or city for which he may be chosen. No person shall be a Senator who, at the time of his election, is not a citizen of Kentucky, has not attained the age of thirty years, and has not resided in this State six years next preceding his election, and the last year thereof in the district for which he may be chosen.

Section 33. The first General Assembly after the adoption of this Constitution shall divide the State into thirty-eight Senatorial Districts, and one hundred Representative Districts, as nearly equal in population as may be without dividing any county, except where a county may include more than one district, which districts shall constitute the Senatorial and Representative Districts for ten years. Not more than two counties shall be joined together to form a Representative District: Provided, In doing so the principle requiring every district to be as nearly equal in population as may be shall not be violated. At the expiration of that time, the General Assembly shall then, and every ten years thereafter, redistrict the State according to this rule, and for the purposes expressed in this section. If, in making said districts, inequality of population should be unavoidable, any advantage resulting therefrom shall be given to districts having the largest territory. No part of a county shall be added to another county to make a district, and the counties forming a district shall be contiguous.

Section 34. The House of Representatives shall choose its Speaker and other officers, and the Senate shall have power to choose its officers biennially.

Section 35. The number of Representatives shall be one hundred, and the number of Senators thirty-eight.

Section 36.

(1) The General Assembly, in odd-numbered years, shall meet in regular session for a period not to exceed a total of thirty (30) legislative days divided as follows: The General Assembly shall convene for the first part of the session on the first Tuesday after the first Monday in January in odd-numbered years for the purposes of electing legislative leaders, adopting rules of procedure, organizing committees, and introducing and considering legislation. The General Assembly shall then adjourn. The General Assembly shall convene for the second part of the session on the first Tuesday in February of that year. Any legislation introduced but not enacted in the first part of the session shall be carried over into the second part of the session. In any part of the session in an odd-numbered year, no bill raising revenue or appropriating funds shall become a law unless it shall be agreed to by three-fifths of all the members elected to each House.

(2) The General Assembly shall then adjourn until the first Tuesday after the first Monday in January of the following even-numbered years, at which time the General Assembly shall convene in regular session.

(3) All sessions shall be held at the seat of government, except in case of war, insurrection or pestilence, when it may, by proclamation of the Governor, assemble, for the time being, elsewhere.

Section 37. Not less than a majority of the members of each House of the General Assembly shall constitute a quorum to do business, but a smaller number may adjourn from day to day, and shall be authorized by law to compel the attendance of absent members in such manner and under such penalties as may be prescribed by law.

Section 38. Each House of the General Assembly shall judge of the qualifications, elections and returns of its members, but a contested election shall be determined in such manner as shall be directed by law.

Section 39. Each House of the General Assembly may determine the rules of its proceedings, punish a member for disorderly behavior, and, with the concurrence of two-thirds, expel a member, but not a second time for the same cause, and may punish for contempt any person who refuses to attend as a witness, or to bring any paper proper to be used as evidence before the General Assembly, or either House thereof, or a Committee of either, or to testify concerning any matter which may be a proper subject of inquiry by the General Assembly, or offers or gives a bribe to a member of the General Assembly, or attempts by other corrupt means or device to control or influence a member to cast his vote or withhold the same. The punishment and mode of proceeding for contempt in such cases shall be prescribed by law, but the term of imprisonment in any such case shall not extend beyond the session of the General Assembly.

Section 40. Each House of the General Assembly shall keep and publish daily a journal of its proceedings; and the yeas and nays of the members on any question shall, at the desire of any two of the members elected, be entered on the journal.

Section 41. Neither House, during the session of the General Assembly, shall, without the consent of the other, adjourn for more than three days, nor to any other place than that in which it may be sitting.

Section 42. The members of the General Assembly shall severally receive from the State Treasury compensation for their services: Provided, No change shall take effect during the session at which it is made; nor shall a session occurring in odd-numbered years extend beyond March 30; nor shall a session of the General Assembly continue beyond sixty legislative days nor shall it extend beyond April 15; these limitations as to length of session shall not apply to the Senate when sitting as a court of impeachment. A legislative day shall be construed to mean a calendar day, exclusive of Sundays, legal holidays, or any day on which neither House meets.

Section 43. The members of the General Assembly shall, in all cases except treason, felony, breach or surety of the peace, be privileged from arrest during their attendance on the sessions of their respective Houses, and in going to and returning from the same; and for any speech or debate in either House they shall not be questioned in any other place.

Section 44. No Senator or Representative shall, during the term for which he was elected, nor for one year thereafter, be appointed or elected to any civil office of profit in this Commonwealth, which shall have been created, or the emoluments of which shall have been increased, during the said term, except to such offices as may be filled by the election of the people.

Section 45. No person who may have been a collector of taxes or public moneys for the Commonwealth, or for any county, city, town or district, or the assistant or deputy of such collector, shall be eligible to the General Assembly, unless he shall have obtained a quietus six months before the election for the amount of such collection, and for all public moneys for which he may have been responsible.

Section 46. No bill shall be considered for final passage unless the same has been reported by a committee and printed for the use of the members. Every bill shall be read at length on three different days in each House, but the second and third readings may be dispensed with by a majority of all the members elected to the House in which the bill is pending. But whenever a committee refuses or fails to report a bill submitted to it in a reasonable time, the same may be called up by any member, and be considered in the same manner it would have been considered if it had been reported. No bill shall become a law unless, on its final passage, it receives the votes of at least two-fifths of the members elected to each House, and a majority of the members voting, the vote to be taken by yeas and nays and entered in the journal: Provided, Any act or resolution for the appropriation of money or the creation of debt shall, on its final passage, receive the votes of a majority of all the members elected to each House.

Section 47. All bills for raising revenue shall originate in the House of Representatives, but the Senate may propose amendments thereto: Provided, No new matter shall be introduced, under color of amendment, which does not relate to raising revenue.

Section 48. The General Assembly shall have no power to enact laws to diminish the resources of the Sinking Fund as now established by law until the debt of the Commonwealth be paid, but may enact laws to increase them; and the whole resources of said fund, from year to year, shall be sacredly set apart and applied to the payment of the interest and principal of the State debt, and to no other use or purpose, until the whole debt of the State is fully satisfied.

Section 49. The General Assembly may contract debts to meet casual deficits or failures in the revenue; but such debts, direct or contingent, singly or in the aggregate, shall not at any time exceed five hundred thousand dollars, and the moneys arising from loans creating such debts shall be applied only to the purpose or purposes for which they were obtained, or to repay such debts: Provided, The General Assembly may contract debts to repel invasion, suppress insurrection, or, if hostilities are threatened, provide for the public defense.

Section 50. No act of the General Assembly shall authorize any debt to be contracted on behalf of the Commonwealth except for the purposes mentioned in Section 49, unless provision be made therein to levy and collect an annual tax sufficient to pay the interest stipulated, and to discharge the debt within thirty years; nor shall such act take effect until it shall have been submitted to the people at a general election, and shall have received a majority of all the votes cast for and against it: Provided, The General Assembly may contract debts by borrowing money to pay any part of the debt of the State, without submission to the people, and without making provision in the act authorizing the same for a tax to discharge the debt so contracted, or the interest thereon.

Section 51. No law enacted by the General Assembly shall relate to more than one subject, and that shall be expressed in the title, and no law shall be revised, amended, or the provisions thereof extended or conferred by reference to its title only, but so much thereof as is revised, amended, extended or conferred, shall be reenacted and published at length.

Section 52. The General Assembly shall have no power to release, extinguish or authorize the releasing or extinguishing, in whole or in part, the indebtedness or liability of any corporation or individual to this Commonwealth, or to any county or municipality thereof.

Section 53. The General Assembly shall provide by law for monthly investigations into the accounts of the Treasurer and Auditor of Public Accounts, and the result of these investigations shall be reported to the Governor, and these reports shall be semiannually published in two newspapers of general circulation in the State. The reports received by the Governor shall, at the beginning of each session, be transmitted by him to the General Assembly for scrutiny and appropriate action.

Section 54. The General Assembly shall have no power to limit the amount to be recovered for injuries resulting in death, or for injuries to person or property.

Section 55. No act, except general appropriation bills, shall become a law until ninety days after the adjournment of the session at which it was passed, except in cases of emergency, when, by the concurrence of a majority of the members elected to each House of the General Assembly, by a yea and nay vote entered upon their journals, an act may become a law when approved by the Governor; but the reasons for the emergency that justifies this action must be set out at length in the journal of each House.

Section 56. No bill shall become a law until the same shall have been signed by the presiding officer of each of the two Houses in open session; and before such officer shall have affixed his signature to any bill, he shall suspend all other business, declare that such bill will now be read, and that he will sign the same to the end that it may become a law. The bill shall then be read at length and compared; and, if correctly enrolled, he shall, in the presence of the House in open session, and before any other business is entertained, affix his signature, which fact shall be noted in the journal, and the bill immediately sent to the other House. When it reaches the other House, the presiding officer thereof shall immediately suspend all other business, announce the reception of the bill, and the same proceeding shall thereupon be observed in every respect as in the House in which it was first signed. And thereupon the Clerk of the latter House shall immediately present the same to the Governor for his signature and approval.

Section 57. A member who has a personal or private interest in any measure or bill proposed or pending before the General Assembly, shall disclose the fact to the House of which he is a member, and shall not vote thereon upon pain of expulsion.

Section 58. The General Assembly shall neither audit nor allow any private claim against the Commonwealth, except for expenses incurred during the session at which the same was allowed; but may appropriate money to pay such claim as shall have been audited and allowed according to law.

Section 59. The General Assembly shall not pass local or special acts concerning any of the following subjects, or for any of the following purposes, namely:

First: To regulate the jurisdiction, or the practice, or the circuits of the courts of justice, or the rights, powers, duties or compensation of the officers thereof; but the practice in circuit courts in continuous session may, by a general law, be made different from the practice of circuit courts held in terms.

Second: To regulate the summoning, impaneling or compensation of grand or petit jurors.

Third: To provide for changes of venue in civil or criminal causes.

Fourth: To regulate the punishment of crimes and misdemeanors, or to remit fines, penalties or forfeitures.

Fifth: To regulate the limitation of civil or criminal causes.

Sixth: To affect the estate of cestuis que trust, decedents, infants or other persons under disabilities, or to authorize any such persons to sell, lease, encumber or dispose of their property.

Seventh: To declare any person of age, or to relieve an infant or feme covert of disability, or to enable him to do acts allowed only to adults not under disabilities.

Eighth: To change the law of descent, distribution or succession.

Ninth: To authorize the adoption or legitimation of children.

Tenth: To grant divorces.

Eleventh: To change the names of persons.

Twelfth: To give effect to invalid deeds, wills or other instruments.

Thirteenth: To legalize, except as against the Commonwealth, the unauthorized or invalid act of any officer or public agent of the Commonwealth, or of any city, county or municipality thereof.

Fourteenth: To refund money legally paid into the State Treasury.

Fifteenth: To authorize or to regulate the levy, the assessment or the collection of taxes, or to give any indulgence or discharge to any assessor or collector of taxes, or to his sureties.

Sixteenth: To authorize the opening, altering, maintaining or vacating of roads, highways, streets, alleys, town plats, cemeteries, graveyards, or public grounds not owned by the Commonwealth.

Seventeenth: To grant a charter to any corporation, or to amend the charter of any existing corporation; to license companies or persons to own or operate ferries, bridges, roads or turnpikes; to declare streams navigable, or to authorize the construction of booms or dams therein, or to remove obstructions therefrom; to affect toll gates or to regulate tolls; to regulate fencing or the running at large of stock.

Eighteenth: To create, increase or decrease fees, percentages or allowances to public officers, or to extend the time for the collection thereof, or to authorize officers to appoint deputies.

Nineteenth: To give any person or corporation the right to lay a railroad track or tramway, or to amend existing charters for such purposes.

Twentieth: To provide for conducting elections, or for designating the places of voting, or changing the boundaries of wards, precincts or districts, except when new counties may be created.

Twenty-first: To regulate the rate of interest.

Twenty-second: To authorize the creation, extension, enforcement, impairment or release of liens.

Twenty-third: To provide for the protection of game and fish.

Twenty-fourth: To regulate labor, trade, mining or manufacturing.

Twenty-fifth: To provide for the management of common schools.

Twenty-sixth: To locate or change a county seat.

Twenty-seventh: To provide a means of taking the sense of the people of any city, town, district, precinct or county, whether they wish to authorize, regulate or prohibit therein the sale of vinous, spirituous or malt liquors, or alter the liquor laws.

Twenty-eighth: Restoring to citizenship persons convicted of infamous crimes.

Twenty-ninth: In all other cases where a general law can be made applicable, no special law shall be enacted.

Section 60. The General Assembly shall not indirectly enact any special or local act by the repeal in part of a general act, or by exempting from the operation of a general act any city, town, district or county; but laws repealing local or special acts may be enacted. No law shall be enacted granting powers or privileges in any case where the granting of such powers or privileges shall have been provided for by a general law, nor where the courts have jurisdiction to grant the same or to give the relief asked for. No law, except such as relates to the sale, loan or gift of vinous, spirituous or malt liquors, bridges, turnpikes or other public roads, public buildings or improvements, fencing, running at large of stock, matters pertaining to common schools, paupers, and the regulation by counties, cities, towns or other municipalities of their local affairs, shall be enacted to take effect upon the approval of any other authority than the General Assembly, unless otherwise expressly provided in this Constitution.[

Section 61. The General Assembly shall, by general law, provide a means whereby the sense of the people of any county, city, town, district or precinct may be taken, as to whether or not spirituous, vinous or malt liquors shall be sold, bartered or loaned therein, or the sale thereof regulated. But nothing herein shall be construed to nterfere with or to repeal any law in force relating to the sale or gift of such liquors. All elections on this question may be held on a day other than the regular election days.

Section 62. The style of the laws of this Commonwealth shall be as follows: "Be it enacted by the General Assembly of the Commonwealth of Kentucky."

Counties and County Seats

Section 63. No new county shall be created by the General Assembly which will reduce the county or counties, or either of them, from which it shall be taken, to less area than four hundred square miles; nor shall any county be formed of less area; nor shall any boundary line thereof pass within less than ten miles of any county seat of the county or counties proposed to be divided. Nothing contained herein shall prevent the General Assembly from abolishing any county.[

Section 64. No county shall be divided, or have any part stricken therefrom, except in the formation of new counties, without submitting the question to a vote of the people of the county, nor unless the majority of all the legal voters of the county voting on the question shall vote for the same. The county seat of no county as now located, or as may hereafter be located, shall be moved, except upon a vote of two-thirds of those voting; nor shall any new county be established which will reduce any county to less than twelve thousand inhabitants, nor shall any county be created containing a less population.

Section 65. There shall be no territory stricken from any county unless a majority of the voters living in such territory shall petition for such division. But the portion so stricken off and added to another county, or formed in whole or in part into a new county, shall be bound for its proportion of the indebtedness of the county from which it has been taken.

Impeachments

Section 66. The House of Representatives shall have the sole power of impeachment.

Section 67. All impeachments shall be tried by the Senate. When sitting for that purpose, the Senators shall be upon oath or affirmation. No person shall be convicted without the concurrence of two-thirds of the Senators present.

Section 68. The Governor and all civil officers shall be liable to impeachment for any misdemeanors in office; but judgment in such cases shall not extend further than removal from office, and disqualification to hold any office of honor, trust or profit under this Commonwealth; but the party convicted shall, nevertheless, be subject and liable to indictment, trial and punishment by law.

The Executive Department

Officers of the State at Large:

Section 69. The supreme executive power of the Commonwealth shall be vested in a Chief Magistrate, who shall be styled the "Governor of the Commonwealth of Kentucky."

Section 70. The Governor and Lieutenant Governor shall be elected for the term of four years by the qualified voters of the State. They shall be elected jointly by the casting by each voter of a single vote applicable to both offices, as shall be provided by law. The slate of candidates having the highest number of votes cast jointly for them for Governor and Lieutenant Governor shall be elected; but if two or more slates of candidates shall be equal and highest in votes, the election shall be determined by lot in such manner as the General Assembly may direct.

Section 71. The Governor shall be ineligible for the succeeding four years after the expiration of any second consecutive term for which he shall have been elected.

Section 72. The Governor and the Lieutenant Governor shall be at least thirty years of age, and have been citizens and residents of Kentucky for at least six years next preceding their election. The duties of the Lieutenant Governor shall be prescribed by law, and he shall have such other duties as delegated by the Governor.

Section 73. The Governor and the Lieutenant Governor shall commence the execution of the duties of their offices on the fifth Tuesday succeeding their election, and shall continue in the execution thereof until a successor shall have qualified.

Section 74. The Governor and Lieutenant Governor shall at stated times receive for the performance of the duties of their respective offices compensation to be fixed by law.

Section 75. He shall be Commander-in-Chief of the army and navy of this Commonwealth, and of the militia thereof, except when they shall be called into the service of the United States; but he shall not command personally in the field, unless advised so to do by a resolution of the General Assembly.

Section 76. He shall have the power, except as otherwise provided in this Constitution, to fill vacancies by granting commissions, which shall expire when such vacancies shall have been filled according to the provisions of this Constitution.

Section 77. He shall have power to remit fines and forfeitures, commute sentences, grant reprieves and pardons, except in case of impeachment, and he shall file with each application therefore a statement of the reasons for his decision thereon, which application and statement shall always be open to public inspection. In cases of treason, he shall have power to grant reprieves until the end of the next session of the General Assembly, in which the power of pardoning shall be vested; but he shall have no power to remit the fees of the Clerk, Sheriff or Commonwealth's Attorney in penal or criminal cases.

Section 78. He may require information in writing from the officers of the Executive Department upon any subject relating to the duties of their respective offices.

Section 79. He shall, from time to time, give to the General Assembly information of the state of the Commonwealth, and recommend to their consideration such measures as he may deem expedient.

Section 80. He may, on extraordinary occasions, convene the General Assembly at the seat of government, or at a different place, if that should have become dangerous from an enemy or from contagious diseases. In case of disagreement between the two Houses with respect to the time of adjournment, he may adjourn them to such time as he shall think proper, not exceeding four months. When he shall convene the General

Assembly it shall be by proclamation, stating the subjects to be considered, and no other shall be considered.

Section 81. He shall take care that the laws be faithfully executed.

Section 82. The Lieutenant Governor shall be ineligible to the office of Lieutenant Governor for the succeeding four (4) years after the expiration of any second consecutive term for which he shall have been elected.

Section 83. Repealed.

Section 84. Should the Governor be impeached and removed from office, die, refuse to qualify, resign, certify by entry on his Journal that he is unable to discharge the duties of his office, or be, from any cause, unable to discharge the duties of his office, the Lieutenant Governor shall exercise all the power and authority appertaining to the office of Governor until another be duly elected and qualified, or the Governor shall be able to discharge the duties of his office. On the trial of the Governor, the President of the Senate shall not preside over the proceedings, but the Chief Justice of the Supreme Court shall preside during the trial.

If the Governor, due to physical or mental incapacitation, is unable to discharge the duties of his office, the Attorney General may petition the Supreme Court to have the Governor declared disabled. If the Supreme Court determines in a unanimous decision that the Governor is unable to discharge the duties of his office, the Chief Justice shall certify such disability to the Secretary of State who shall enter same on the Journal of the Acts of the Governor, and the Lieutenant Governor shall assume the duties of the Governor, and shall act as Governor until the Supreme Court determines that the disability of the Governor has ceased to exist. Before the Governor resumes his duties, the finding of the Court that the disability has ceased shall be certified by the Chief Justice to the Secretary of State who shall enter such finding on the Journal of the Acts of the Governor.

Section 85. A President of the Senate shall be elected by each Senate as soon after its organization as possible and as often as there is a vacancy in the office of President, another President of the Senate shall be elected by the Senate, if in session. And if, during the vacancy of the office of Governor, the Lieutenant Governor shall be impeached and removed from office, refuse to qualify, resign, or die, the President of the Senate shall in like manner administer the government.

Section 86. The President of the Senate shall receive for his services the same compensation which shall, for the same period, be allowed to the Speaker of the House of Representatives, and during the time he administers the government as Governor, he shall receive the same compensation which the Governor would have received had he been employed in the duties of his office.

Section 87. If the Lieutenant Governor shall be called upon to administer the government in place of the Governor, and shall, while in such administration, resign, or die during the recess of the General Assembly, if there be no President of the Senate, it shall be the duty of the Attorney General, for the time being, to convene the Senate for the purpose of choosing a President; and until a President is chosen, the Attorney General shall administer the government. If there be no Attorney General to perform the duties devolved upon him by this section, then the Auditor, for the time being, shall convene the Senate for the purpose of choosing a President, and shall administer the government until a President is chosen.

Section 88. Every bill which shall have passed the two Houses shall be presented to the Governor. If he approve, he shall sign it; but if not, he shall return it, with his objections, to the House in which it originated, which shall enter the objections in full upon its journal, and proceed to reconsider it. If, after such reconsideration, a majority of all the members elected to that

House shall agree to pass the bill, it shall be sent, with the objections, to the other House, by which it shall likewise be considered, and if approved by a majority of all the members elected to that House, it shall be a law; but in such case the votes of both Houses shall be determined by yeas and nays, and the names of the members voting for and against the bill shall be entered upon the journal of each House respectively. If any bill shall not be returned by the Governor within ten days (Sundays excepted) after it shall have been presented to him, it shall be a law in like manner as if he had signed it, unless the General Assembly, by their adjournment, prevent its return, in which case it shall be a law, unless disapproved by him within ten days after the adjournment, in which case his veto message shall be spread upon the register kept by the Secretary of State. The Governor shall have the power to disapprove any part or parts of appropriation bills embracing distinct items, and the part or parts disapproved shall not become a law unless reconsidered and passed, as in case of a bill.

Section 89. Every order, resolution or vote, in which the concurrence of both Houses may be necessary, except on a question of adjournment, or as otherwise provided in this Constitution, shall be presented to the Governor, and, before it shall take effect, be approved by him; or, being disapproved, shall be repassed by a majority of the members elected to both Houses, according to the rules and limitations prescribed in case of a bill.

Section 90. Contested elections for Governor and Lieutenant Governor shall be determined by both Houses of the General Assembly, according to such regulations as may be established by law.

Section 91. A Treasurer, Auditor of Public Accounts, Commissioner of Agriculture, Labor and Statistics, Secretary of State, and Attorney-General, shall be elected by the qualified voters of the State at the same time the Governor and Lieutenant Governor are elected, for the term of four years, each of whom shall be at least thirty years of age at the time of his election, and shall have been a resident citizen of the State at least two years next before his election. The duties of all these officers shall be such as may be prescribed by law, and the Secretary of State shall keep a fair register of and attest all the official acts of the Governor, and shall, when required, lay the same and all papers, minutes and vouchers relative thereto before either House of the General Assembly. The officers named in this section shall enter upon the discharge of their duties the first Monday in January after their election, and shall hold their offices until their successors are elected and qualified.

Section 92. The Attorney-General shall have been a practicing lawyer eight years before his election.

Section 93. The Treasurer, Auditor of Public Accounts, Secretary of State, Commissioner of Agriculture, Labor and Statistics, and Attorney General shall be ineligible to re-election for the succeeding four years after the expiration of any second consecutive term for which they shall have been elected. The duties and responsibilities of these officers shall be prescribed by law, and all fees collected by any of said officers shall be covered into the treasury. Inferior State officers and members of boards and commissions, not specifically provided for in this Constitution, may be appointed or elected, in such manner as may be prescribed by law, which may include a requirement of consent by the Senate, for a term not exceeding four years, and until their successors are appointed or elected and qualified.

Section 94. Repealed.

Section 95. The election under this Constitution for Governor, Lieutenant Governor, Treasurer, Auditor of Public Accounts, Attorney General, Secretary of State, and Commissioner of Agriculture, Labor and Statistics, shall be held on the first Tuesday after the first Monday in November, eighteen hundred and ninety-five, and the same day every four years thereafter.

Section 96. All officers mentioned in Section 95 shall be paid for their services by salary, and not otherwise.

Officers for Districts and Counties:

Section 97. In the year two thousand, and every six years thereafter, there shall be an election in each county for a Circuit Court Clerk, and for a Commonwealth's Attorney, in each circuit court district, unless that office be abolished, who shall hold their respective offices for six years from the first Monday in January after their election, and until the election and qualification of their successors.

Section 98. The compensation of the Commonwealth's Attorney shall be by salary and such percentage of fines and forfeitures as may be fixed by law, and such salary shall be uniform in so far as the same shall be paid out of the State Treasury, and not to exceed the sum of five hundred dollars per annum; but any county may make additional compensation, to be paid by said county. Should any percentage of fines and forfeitures be allowed by law, it shall not be paid except upon such proportion of fines and forfeitures as have been collected and paid into the State Treasury, and not until so collected and paid.

Section 99. At the regular election in nineteen hundred and ninety-eight and every four years thereafter, there shall be elected in each county a Judge of the County Court, a County Court Clerk, a County Attorney, Sheriff, Jailer, Coroner, Surveyor and Assessor, and in each Justice's District one Justice of the Peace and one Constable, who shall enter upon the discharge of the duties of their offices on the first Monday in January after their election, and who shall hold their offices four years until the election and qualification of their successors.

Section 100. No person shall be eligible to the offices mentioned in Sections 97 and 99 who is not at the time of his election twenty-four years of age (except Clerks of County and Circuit Courts, who shall be twenty-one years of age), a citizen of Kentucky, and who has not resided in the State two years, and one year next preceding his election in the county and district in which he is a candidate. No person shall be eligible to the office of Commonwealth's Attorney unless he shall have been a licensed practicing lawyer four years. No person shall be eligible to the office of County Attorney unless he shall have been a licensed practicing lawyer two years. No person shall be eligible to the office of Clerk unless he shall have procured from a Judge of the Court of Appeals, or a Judge of a Circuit Court, a certificate that he has been examined by the Clerk of his Court under his supervision, and that he is qualified for the office for which he is a candidate.

Section 101. Constables shall possess the same qualifications as Sheriffs, and their jurisdictions shall be coextensive with the counties in which they reside. Constables now in office shall continue in office until their successors are elected and qualified.

Section 102. When a new county shall be created, officers for the same, to serve until the next regular election, shall be elected or appointed in such way and at such times as the General Assembly may prescribe.

Section 103. The Judges of County Courts, Clerks, Sheriffs, Surveyors, Coroners, Jailers, Constables, and such other officers as the General Assembly may, from time to time, require, shall before they enter upon the duties of their respective offices, and as often thereafter as may be deemed proper, give such bond and security as may be prescribed by law.

Section 104. The General Assembly may abolish the office of Assessor and provide that the assessment of property shall be made by other officers; but it shall have power to reestablish the office of Assessor and prescribe his duties. No person shall be eligible to the office of Assessor two consecutive terms.

Section 105. The General Assembly may, at any time, consolidate the offices of Jailer and Sheriff in any county or counties, as it shall deem most expedient; but in the event such consolidation be made, the office of Sheriff shall be retained, and the Sheriff shall be required to perform the duties of Jailer.

Section 106. The fees of county officers shall be regulated by law. In counties or cities having a population of seventy-five thousand or more, the Clerks of the respective Courts thereof (except the Clerk of the City Court), the Marshals, the Sheriffs and the Jailers, shall be paid out of the State Treasury, by salary to be fixed by law, the salaries of said officers and of their deputies and necessary office expenses not to exceed seventy-five per centum of the fees collected by said officers, respectively, and paid into the Treasury.

Section 107. The General Assembly may provide for the election or appointment, for a term not exceeding four years, of such other county or district ministerial and executive officers as may, from time to time, be necessary.

Section 108. The General Assembly may, at any time after the expiration of six years from the adoption of this Constitution, abolish the office of Commonwealth's Attorney, to take effect upon the expiration of the term of the incumbents, in which event the duties of said office shall be discharged by the County Attorneys.

The Judicial Department:

Section 109. The judicial power of the Commonwealth shall be vested exclusively in one Court of Justice which shall be divided into a Supreme Court, a Court of Appeals, a trial court of general jurisdiction known as the Circuit Court and a trial court of limited jurisdiction known as the District Court. The court shall constitute a unified judicial system for operation and administration. The impeachment powers of the General Assembly shall remain inviolate.

The Supreme Court:

Section 110.

(1) The Supreme Court shall consist of the Chief Justice of the Commonwealth and six associate Justices.

(2) (a) The Supreme Court shall have appellate jurisdiction only, except it shall have the power to issue all writs necessary in aid of its appellate jurisdiction, or the complete determination of any cause, or as may be required to exercise control of the Court of Justice.

(b) Appeals from a judgment of the Circuit Court imposing a sentence of death or life imprisonment or imprisonment for twenty years or more shall be taken directly to the Supreme Court. In all other cases, criminal and civil, the Supreme Court shall exercise appellate jurisdiction as provided by its rules.

(3) A majority of the Justices of the Supreme Court shall constitute a quorum for the transaction of business. If as many as two Justices decline or are unable to sit in the trial of any cause, the Chief Justice shall certify that fact to the Governor, who shall appoint to try the particular cause a sufficient number of Justices to constitute a full court for the trial of the cause.

(4) The Court of Appeals districts existing on the effective date of this amendment to the Constitution shall constitute the initial Supreme Court districts. The General Assembly thereafter may redistrict the Commonwealth, by counties, into seven Supreme Court districts as nearly equal in population and as compact in form as possible. There shall be one Justice from each Supreme Court district.

(5) (a) The Justices of the Supreme Court shall elect one of their number to serve as Chief Justice for a term of four years.

(b) The Chief Justice of the Commonwealth shall be the executive head of the Court of Justice and he shall appoint such administrative assistants as he deems necessary. He shall assign temporarily any justice or judge of the Commonwealth, active or retired, to sit in any court other than the Supreme Court when he deems such assignment necessary for the prompt disposition of causes. The Chief Justice shall submit the budget for the Court of Justice and perform all other necessary administrative functions relating to the court.

The Court of Appeals:

Section 111. **(1)** The Court of Appeals shall consist initially of fourteen judges, an equal number to be selected from each Supreme Court district. The number of judges thereafter shall be determined from time to time by the General Assembly upon certification of necessity by the Supreme Court.

(2) The Court of Appeals shall have appellate jurisdiction only, except that it may be authorized by rules of the Supreme Court to review directly decisions of administrative agencies of the Commonwealth, and it may issue all writs necessary in aid of its appellate jurisdiction, or the complete determination of any cause within its appellate jurisdiction. In all other cases, it shall exercise appellate jurisdiction as provided by law.

(3) The judges of the Court of Appeals shall elect one of their number to serve as Chief Judge for a term of four years. The Chief Judge shall exercise such authority and perform such duties in the administration of the Court of Appeals as are prescribed in this section or as may be prescribed by the Supreme Court.

(4) The Court of Appeals shall divide itself into panels of not less than three judges. A panel may decide a cause by the concurring vote of a majority of its judges. The Chief Judge shall make assignments of judges to panels. The Court of Appeals shall prescribe the times and places in the Commonwealth at which each panel shall sit.

The Circuit Court:

(1) Circuit Court shall be held in each county.

(2) The Circuit Court districts existing on the effective date of this amendment to the Constitution shall continue under the name "Judicial Circuits," the General Assembly having power upon certification of the necessity therefore by the Supreme Court to reduce, increase or rearrange the judicial districts. A judicial circuit composed of more than one county shall be as compact in form as possible and of contiguous counties. No county shall be divided in creating a judicial circuit.

(3) The number of circuit judges in each district existing on the effective date of this amendment shall continue, the General Assembly having power upon certification of the necessity therefore by the Supreme Court, to change the number of circuit judges in any judicial circuit.

(4) In a judicial circuit having only one judge, he shall be the chief judge. In judicial circuits having two or more judges, they shall select biennially a chief judge, and if they fail to do so within a reasonable time, the Supreme Court shall designate the chief judge. The chief judge shall exercise such authority and perform such duties in the administration of his judicial circuit as may be prescribed by the Supreme Court. The Supreme Court may provide by rules for administration of judicial circuits by regions designated by it.

(5) The Circuit Court shall have original jurisdiction of all justiciable causes not vested in some other court. It shall have such appellate jurisdiction as may be provided by law.

(6) The Supreme Court may designate one or more divisions of Circuit Court within a judicial circuit as a family court division. A Circuit Court division so designated shall retain the general jurisdiction of the Circuit Court and shall have additional jurisdiction as may be provided by the General Assembly.

The District Court:

Section 113. **(1)** District Court shall be held in each county.

(2) The Circuit Court districts existing on the effective date of this amendment shall continue for District Court purposes under the name "Judicial Districts," the General Assembly having power upon certification of the necessity therefore by the Supreme Court to reduce, increase or rearrange the districts. A judicial district composed of more than one county shall be as compact in form as possible and of contiguous counties. No county shall be divided in creating a judicial district.

(3) Each judicial district created by this amendment initially shall have at least one district judge who shall serve as chief judge and there shall be such other district judges as the General Assembly shall determine. The number of district judges in each judicial district thereafter shall be determined by the General Assembly upon certification of necessity therefore by the Supreme Court.

(4) In a judicial district having only one judge he shall be the chief judge. In those districts having two or more judges they shall select biennially a chief judge and if they fail to do so within a reasonable time, the Supreme Court shall designate the chief judge. The chief judge shall exercise such authority and perform such duties in the administration of his district as may be prescribed by the Supreme Court.

(5) In any county in which no district judge resides the chief judge of the district shall appoint a trial commissioner who shall be a resident of such county and who shall be an attorney if one is qualified and available. Other trial commissioners with like qualifications may be appointed by the chief judge in any judicial district upon certification of the necessity therefore by the Supreme Court. All trial commissioners shall have power to perform such duties of the district court as may be prescribed by the Supreme Court.

(6) The district court shall be a court of limited jurisdiction and shall exercise original jurisdiction as may be provided by the General Assembly.

Clerks of Courts:

Section 114. **(1)** The Supreme Court shall appoint a clerk to serve as it shall determine.

(2) The Court of Appeals shall appoint a clerk to serve as it shall determine.

(3) The clerks of the Circuit Court shall be elected in the manner provided elsewhere in this Constitution. The clerks of the Circuit Court shall serve as the clerks of the District Court. The clerks of the Circuit Court shall be removable from office by the Supreme Court upon good cause shown.

Appellate Policy -- Rule-Making Power:

Section 115. In all cases, civil and criminal, there shall be allowed as a matter of right at least one appeal to another court, except that the Commonwealth may not appeal from a judgment of acquittal in a criminal case, other than for the purpose of securing a certification of law, and the General Assembly may prescribe that there shall be no appeal from that portion of a judgment dissolving a marriage. Procedural rules shall provide for expeditious and inexpensive appeals. Appeals shall be upon the record and not by trial de novo.

Offices of Justices and Judges:

Section 116. The Supreme Court shall have the power to prescribe rules governing its appellate jurisdiction, rules for the appointment of commissioners and other court personnel, and rules of practice and procedure for the Court of Justice. The Supreme Court shall, by rule, govern admission to the bar and the discipline of members of the bar.

Section 117. Justices of the Supreme Court and judges of the Court of Appeals, Circuit and District Court shall be elected from their respective districts or circuits on a nonpartisan basis as provided by law.

Section 118. (1) A vacancy in the office of a justice of the Supreme Court, or of a judge of the Court of Appeals, circuit or district court which under Section 152 of this Constitution is to be filled by appointment by the Governor shall be filled by the Governor from a list of three names presented to him by the appropriate judicial nominating commission. If the Governor fails to make an appointment from the list within sixty days from the date it is presented to him, the appointment shall be made from the same list by the chief justice of the Supreme Court.

(2) There shall be one judicial nominating commission for the Supreme Court and the Court of Appeals, one for each judicial circuit, and one for each judicial district, except that a circuit and district having the same boundary shall have but one judicial nominating commission. Each commission shall consist of seven members, one of whom shall be the chief justice of the Supreme Court, who shall be chairman. Two members of each commission shall be members of the bar, who shall be elected by their fellow members. The other four members shall be appointed by the Governor from among persons not members of the bar, and these four shall include at least two members of each of the two political parties of the Commonwealth having the largest number of voters. Members of a judicial circuit or judicial district nominating commission must be residents of the circuit or district, respectively, and the lawyer members of the commission shall be elected by the members of the bar residing in the circuit or district, respectively. The terms of office of members of judicial nominating commissions shall be fixed by the General Assembly. No person shall be elected or appointed a member of a judicial nominating commission who holds any other public office or any office in a political party or organization.

Section 119. Justices of the Supreme Court and judges of the Court of Appeals and Circuit Court shall severally hold their offices for terms of eight years, and judges of the District Court for terms of four years. All terms commence on the first Monday in January next succeeding the regular election for the office. No justice or judge may be deprived of his term of office by redistricting, or by a reduction in the number of justices or judges.

Section 120. All justices and judges shall be paid adequate compensation which shall be fixed by the General Assembly. All compensation and necessary expenses of the Court of Justice shall be paid out of the State Treasury. The compensation of a justice or judge shall not be reduced during his term.

Section 121. Subject to rules of procedure to be established by the Supreme Court, and after notice and hearing, any justice of the Supreme Court or judge of the Court of Appeals, Circuit Court or District Court may be retired for disability or suspended without pay or removed for good cause by a commission composed of one judge of the Court of Appeals, selected by that court, one circuit judge and one district judge selected by a majority vote of the circuit judges and district judges, respectively, one member of the bar appointed by its governing body, and two persons, not members of the bench or bar, appointed by the Governor. The commission shall be a state body whose members shall hold office for four-year terms. Its actions shall be subject to judicial review by the Supreme Court.

Section 122. To be eligible to serve as a justice of the Supreme Court or a judge of the Court of Appeals, Circuit Court or District Court a person must be a citizen of the United States, licensed to practice law in the courts of this Commonwealth, and have been a resident of this Commonwealth and of the district from which he is elected for two years next preceding his taking office. In addition, to be eligible to serve as a justice of the Supreme Court or judge of the Court of Appeals or Circuit Court a person must have been a licensed attorney for at least eight years. No district judge shall serve who has not been a licensed attorney for at least two years.

Section 123. During his term of office, no justice of the Supreme Court or judge of the Court of Appeals, Circuit Court or District Court shall engage in the practice of law, or run for elective office other than judicial office, or hold any office in a political party or organization.

Section 124. Any remaining sections of the Constitution of Kentucky as it existed prior to the effective date of this amendment which are in conflict with the provisions of amended Sections 110 through 125 are repealed to the extent of the conflict, but such amended sections are not intended to repeal those parts of Sections 140 and 142 conferring nonjudicial powers and duties upon county judges and justices of the peace. Nothing in such amended sections shall be construed to limit the powers otherwise granted by this Constitution to the county judge as the chief executive, administrative and fiscal officer of the county, or to limit the powers otherwise granted by the Constitution to the justices of the peace or county commissioners as executive, administrative and fiscal officers of a county, or of the fiscal court as a governing body of a county.

Section 125-139. Repealed.

County Courts:

Section 140. There shall be established in each county now existing, or which may be hereafter created, in this State, a Court, to be styled the County Court, to consist of a Judge, who shall be a conservator of the peace, and shall receive such compensation for his services as may be prescribed by law. He shall be commissioned by the Governor, and shall vacate his office by removal from the county in which he may have been elected.

Section 141. Repealed.

Justices of the Peace:

Section 142. Each county now existing, or which may hereafter be created, in this State, shall be laid off into districts in such manner as the General Assembly may direct; but no county shall have less than three nor more than eight districts, in each of which districts one Justice of the Peace shall be elected as provided in Section 99. The General Assembly shall make provisions for regulating the number of said districts from time to time within the limits herein prescribed, and for fixing the boundaries thereof. The jurisdiction of Justices of the Peace shall be coextensive with the county, and shall be equal and uniform throughout the State. Justices of the Peace shall be conservators of the peace. They shall be commissioned by the Governor, and shall vacate their offices by removal from the districts, respectively, in which they may have been elected.

Section 143. Repealed.

Fiscal Courts:

Section 144. Counties shall have a Fiscal Court, which may consist of the Judge of the County Court and the Justices of the Peace, in which Court the Judge of the County Court shall preside, if present; or a county may have three Commissioners, to be elected from the county at large, who, together with the Judge of the County Court, shall constitute the Fiscal Court. A majority of the members of said Court shall constitute a Court for the transaction of business. But where, for county governmental purposes, a city is by law separated from the remainder of the county, such Commissioners may be elected from the part of the county outside of such city.

Suffrage and Elections:

Section 145. Every citizen of the United States of the age of eighteen years who has resided in the state one year, and in the county six months, and the precinct in which he offers to vote sixty days next preceding the election, shall be a voter in said precinct and not elsewhere but the following persons are excepted and shall not have the right to vote.

1. Persons convicted in any court of competent jurisdiction of treason, or felony, or bribery in an election, or of such high misdemeanor as the General Assembly may declare shall operate as an exclusion from the right of suffrage, but persons hereby excluded may be restored to their civil rights by executive pardon.

2. Persons who, at the time of the election, are in confinement under the judgment of a court for some penal offense.

3. Idiots and insane persons.

Section 146. No person in the military, naval or marine service of the United States shall be deemed a resident of this State by reason of being stationed within the same.

Section 147. The General Assembly shall provide by law for the registration of all persons entitled to vote in cities and towns having a population of five thousand or more; and may provide by general law for the registration of other voters in the state. Where registration is required, only persons registered shall have the right to vote. The mode of registration shall be prescribed by the General Assembly. In all elections by persons in a representative capacity, the voting shall be viva voce and made a matter of record; but all elections by the people shall be by secret official ballot, furnished by public authority to the voters at the polls, and marked by each voter in private at the polls, and then and there deposited, or any person absent from the county of his legal residence, or from the state, may be permitted to vote in a manner provided by law. Counties so desiring may use voting machines, these machines to be installed at the expense of such counties. The word "elections" in this section includes the decision of questions submitted to the voters, as well as the choice of officers by them. The General Assembly shall pass all necessary laws to enforce this section, and shall provide that persons illiterate, blind, or in any way disabled may have their ballots marked or voted as herein required.

Section 148. Not more than one election each year shall be held in this State or in any city, town, district, urban-county or county thereof, except as otherwise provided in this Constitution. All regular elections of State, county, city, town, urban-county, or district officers shall be held on the first Tuesday after the first Monday in November. All elections by the people shall be between the hours of six o'clock a.m. and seven o'clock p.m., but the General Assembly may change said hours, and all officers of any election shall be residents and voters in the precinct in which they act. The General Assembly shall provide by law that all employers shall allow employees, under reasonable regulations, at least four hours on election days, in which to cast their votes.

Section 149. Voters, in all cases except treason, felony, breach of surety of the peace, or violation of the election laws, shall be privileged from arrest during their attendance at elections, and while they are going to and returning therefrom.

Section 150. Every person shall be disqualified from holding any office of trust or profit for the term for which he shall have been elected who shall be convicted of having given, or consented to the giving, offer or promise of any money or other thing of value, to procure his election, or to influence the vote of any voter at such election; and if any corporation shall, directly or indirectly, offer, promise or give, or shall authorize, directly or indirectly, any person to offer, promise or give any money or any thing of value to influence the result of any election in this State, or the vote of any voter authorized to vote therein, or who shall afterward reimburse or compensate, in any manner whatever, any person who shall have offered, promised or given any money or other thing of value to influence the result of any election or the vote of any such voter, such corporation, if organized under the laws of this Commonwealth, shall, on conviction thereof, forfeit its charter and all rights, privileges and immunities thereunder; and if chartered by another State and doing business in this State, whether by license, or upon mere sufferance, such corporation, upon conviction of either of the offenses aforesaid, shall forfeit all right to carry on any business in this State; and it shall be the duty of the General Assembly to provide for the enforcement of the provisions of this section. All persons shall be excluded from office who have been, or shall hereafter be, convicted of a felony, or of such high misdemeanor as may be prescribed by law, but such disability may be removed by pardon of the Governor. The privilege of free suffrage shall be supported by laws regulating elections, and prohibiting, under adequate penalties, all undue influence thereon, from power, bribery, tumult or other improper practices.

Section 151. The General Assembly shall provide suitable means for depriving of office any person who, to procure his nomination or election, has, in his canvass or election, been guilty of any unlawful use of money, or other thing of value, or has been guilty of fraud, intimidation, bribery, or any other corrupt practice, and he shall be held responsible for acts done by others with his authority, or ratified by him.

Section 152. Except as otherwise provided in this Constitution, vacancies in all elective offices shall be filled by election or appointment, as follows: If the unexpired term will end at the next succeeding annual election at which either city, town, county, district or State officers are to be elected, the office shall be filled by appointment for the remainder of the term. If the unexpired term will not end at the next succeeding annual election at which either city, town, county, district or State officers are to be elected, and if three months intervene before said succeeding annual election at which either city, town, county, district or State officers are to be elected, the office shall be filled by appointment until said election, and then said vacancy shall be filled by election for the remainder of the term. If three months do not intervene between the happening of said vacancy and the next succeeding election at which city, town, county, district or State officers are to be elected, the office shall be filled by appointment until the second succeeding annual election at which city, town, county, district or State officers are to be elected; and then, if any part of the term remains unexpired, the office shall be filled by election until the regular time for the election of officers to fill said offices. Vacancies in all offices for the State at large, or for districts larger than a county, shall be filled by appointment of the Governor; all other appointments shall be made as may be prescribed by law. No person shall ever be appointed a member of the General Assembly, but vacancies therein may be filled at a special election, in such manner as may be provided by law.

Section 153. Except as otherwise herein expressly provided, the General Assembly shall have power to provide by general law for the manner of voting, for ascertaining the result of elections and making due returns thereof, for issuing certificates or commissions to all persons entitled thereto, and for the trial of contested elections.

Section 154. The General Assembly shall prescribe such laws as may be necessary for the restriction or prohibition of the sale or gift of spirituous, vinous or malt liquors on election days.

Section 155. The provisions of Sections 145 to 154, inclusive, shall not apply to the election of school trustees and other common school district elections. Said elections shall be regulated by the General Assembly, except as otherwise provided in this Constitution.

Municipalities:

Section 156. Repealed.

Section 156a. The General Assembly may provide for the creation, alteration of boundaries, consolidation, merger, dissolution, government, functions, and officers of cities. The General Assembly shall create such classifications of cities as it deems necessary based on population, tax base, form of government, geography, or any other reasonable basis and enact legislation relating to the classifications. All legislation relating to cities of a certain classification shall apply equally to all cities within the same classification. The classification of all cities and the law pertaining to the classifications in effect at the time of adoption of this section shall remain in effect until otherwise provided by law.

Section 156b. The General Assembly may provide by general law that cities may exercise any power and perform any function within their boundaries that is in furtherance of a public purpose of a city and not in conflict with a constitutional provision or statute.

Section 157. The tax rate of cities, counties, and taxing districts, for other than school purposes, shall not, at any time, exceed the following rates upon the value of the taxable property therein: For all cities having a population of fifteen thousand or more, one dollar and fifty cents on the hundred dollars; for all cities having less than fifteen thousand and not less than ten thousand, one dollar on the hundred dollars; for all cities having less than ten thousand, seventy-five cents on the hundred dollars; and for counties and taxing districts, fifty cents on the hundred dollars.

Section 157a. The credit of the Commonwealth may be given, pledged or loaned to any county of the Commonwealth for public road purposes, and any county may be permitted to incur an indebtedness in any amount fixed by the county, not in excess of five per centum of the value of the taxable property therein, for public road purposes in said county, provided said additional indebtedness is submitted to the voters of the county for their ratification or rejection at a special election held for said purpose, in such manner as may be provided by law and when any such indebtedness is incurred by any county said county may levy, in addition to the tax rate allowed under Section 157 of the Constitution of Kentucky, an amount not exceeding twenty cents on the one hundred dollars of the assessed valuation of said county for the purpose of paying the interest on said indebtedness and providing a sinking fund for the payment of said indebtedness.

Section 157b. Prior to each fiscal year, the legislative body of each city, county, and taxing district shall adopt a budget showing total expected revenues and expenditures for the fiscal year. No city, county, or taxing district shall expend any funds in any fiscal year in excess of the revenues for that fiscal year. A city, county, or taxing district may amend its budget for a fiscal year, but the revised expenditures may not exceed the revised revenues. As used in this section, "revenues" shall mean all income from every source, including unencumbered reserves carried over from the previous fiscal year, and "expenditures" shall mean all funds to be paid out for expenses of the city, county, or taxing district during the fiscal year, including amounts necessary to pay the principal and interest due during the fiscal year on any debt.

Section 158. Cities, towns, counties, and taxing districts shall not incur indebtedness to an amount exceeding the following maximum percentages on the value of the taxable property therein, to be estimated by the last assessment previous to the incurring of the indebtedness: Cities having a population of fifteen thousand or more, ten percent (10%); cities having a population of less than fifteen thousand but not less than three thousand, five percent (5%); cities having a population of less than three thousand, three percent (3%); and counties and taxing districts, two percent (2%), unless in case of emergency, the public health or safety should so require. Nothing shall prevent the issue of renewal bonds, or bonds to fund the floating indebtedness of any city, county, or taxing district. Subject to the limits and conditions set forth in this section and elsewhere in this Constitution, the General Assembly shall have the power to establish additional limits on indebtedness and conditions under which debt may be incurred by cities, counties, and taxing districts.

Section 159. Whenever any city, town, county, taxing district or other municipality is authorized to contract an indebtedness, it shall be required, at the same time, to provide for the collection of an annual tax sufficient to pay the interest on said indebtedness, and to create a sinking fund for the payment of the principal thereof, within not more than forty years from the time of contracting the same.

Section 160. The Mayor or Chief Executive, Police Judges, members of legislative boards or councils of towns and cities shall be elected by the qualified voters thereof: Provided, The Mayor or Chief Executive and Police Judges of the towns of the fourth, fifth and sixth classes may be appointed or elected as provided by law. The terms of office of Mayors or Chief Executives and Police Judges shall be four years, and until their successors shall be qualified, and of members of legislative boards, two years. When any city of the first or second class is divided into wards or districts, members of legislative boards shall be elected at large by the qualified voters of said city, but so selected that an equal proportion thereof shall reside in each of the said wards or districts; but when in any city of the first, second or third class, there are two legislative boards, the less numerous shall be selected from and elected by the voters at large of said city; but other officers of towns or cities shall be elected by the qualified voters therein, or appointed by the local authorities thereof, as the General Assembly may, by a general law, provide; but when elected by the voters of a town or city, their terms of office shall be four years, and until their successors shall be qualified. No Mayor or Chief Executive of any city of the first or second class, after the expiration of three successive terms of office to which he has been elected under this Constitution shall be eligible for the succeeding term. No fiscal officer of any city of the first or second class, after the expiration of the term of office to which he has been elected under this Constitution, shall be eligible for the succeeding term. "Fiscal officer" shall not include an Auditor or Assessor, or any other officer whose chief duty is not the collection or holding of public moneys. The General Assembly shall prescribe the qualifications of all officers of towns and cities, the manner in and causes for which they may be removed from office, and how vacancies in such offices may be filled.

Section 161. The compensation of any city, county, town or municipal officer shall not be changed after his election or appointment, or during his term of office; nor shall the term of any such officer be extended beyond the period for which he may have been elected or appointed.

Section 162. No county, city, town or other municipality shall ever be authorized or permitted to pay any claim created against it, under any agreement or contract made without express authority of law, and all such unauthorized agreements or contracts shall be null and void.

Section 163. No street railway, gas, water, steam heating, telephone, or electric light company, within a city or town, shall be permitted or authorized to construct its tracks, lay its pipes or mains, or erect its poles, posts or other apparatus along, over, under or across the streets, alleys or public grounds of a city or town, without the consent of the proper legislative bodies or boards of such city or town being first obtained; but when charters have been heretofore granted conferring such rights, and work has in good faith been begun thereunder, the provisions of this section shall not apply.

Section 164. No county, city, town, taxing district or other municipality shall be authorized or permitted to grant any franchise or privilege, or make any contract in reference thereto, for a term exceeding twenty years. Before granting such franchise or privilege for a term of years, such municipality shall first, after due advertisement, receive bids therefore publicly, and award the same to the highest and best bidder; but it shall have the right to reject any or all bids. This section shall not apply to a trunk railway.

Section 165. No person shall, at the same time, be a State officer or a deputy officer or member of the General Assembly, and an officer of any county, city, town, or other municipality, or an employee thereof; and no person shall, at the same time, fill two municipal offices, either in the same or different municipalities, except as may be otherwise provided in this Constitution; but a Notary Public, or an officer of the militia, shall not be ineligible to hold any other office mentioned in this section.

Section 166. All acts of incorporation of cities and towns heretofore granted, and all amendments thereto, except as provided in Section 167, shall continue in force under this Constitution, and all City and Police Courts established in any city or town shall remain, with their present powers and jurisdictions, until such time as the General Assembly shall provide by general laws for the government of towns and cities, and the officers and courts thereof; but not longer than four years from and after the first day of January, one thousand eight hundred and ninety-one, within which time the General Assembly shall provide by general laws for the government of towns and cities, and the officers and courts thereof, as provided in this Constitution.

Section 167. All officers required to be elected in cities, urban-counties, and towns by this Constitution, or by general laws enacted in conformity to its provisions, shall be elected at the general elections in November in even-numbered years.

Section 168. No municipal ordinance shall fix a penalty for a violation thereof at less than that imposed by statute for the same offense. A conviction or acquittal under either shall constitute a bar to another prosecution for the same offense.

Revenue and Taxation:

Section 169. The fiscal year shall commence on the first day of July in each year, unless otherwise provided by law.

Section 170. There shall be exempt from taxation public property used for public purposes; places of burial not held for private or corporate profit; real property owned and occupied by, and personal property both tangible and intangible owned by, institutions of religion; institutions of purely public charity, and institutions of education not used or employed for gain by any person or corporation, and the income of which is devoted solely to the cause of education, public libraries, their endowments, and the income of such property as is used exclusively for their maintenance; household goods of a person used in his home; crops grown in the year in which the assessment is made, and in the hands of the producer; and real property maintained as the permanent residence of the owner, who is sixty-five years of age or older, or is classified as totally disabled under a program authorized or administered by an agency of the United States government or by any retirement system either within or without the Commonwealth of Kentucky, provided the property owner received disability payments pursuant to such disability classification, has maintained such disability classification for the entirety of the particular taxation period, and has filed with the appropriate local assessor by December 31 of the taxation period, on forms provided therefore, a signed statement indicating continuing disability as provided herein made under penalty of perjury, up to the assessed valuation of sixty-five hundred dollars on said residence and contiguous real property, except for assessment for special benefits. The real property may be held by legal or equitable title, by the entireties, jointly, in common, as a condominium, or indirectly by the stock ownership or membership representing the owner's or member's proprietary interest in a corporation owning a fee or a leasehold initially in excess of ninety-eight years. The exemptions shall apply only to the value of the real property assessable to the owner or, in case of ownership through stock or membership in a corporation, the value of the proportion which his interest in the corporation bears to the assessed value of the property. The General Assembly may authorize any incorporated city or town to exempt manufacturing establishments from municipal taxation, for a period not exceeding five years, as an inducement to their location. Notwithstanding the provisions of Sections 3, 172, and 174 of this Constitution to the contrary, the General Assembly may provide by law an exemption for all or any portion of the property tax for any class of personal property.

Section 171. The General Assembly shall provide by law an annual tax, which, with other resources, shall be sufficient to defray the estimated expenses of the Commonwealth for each fiscal year. Taxes shall be levied and collected for public purposes only and shall be uniform upon all property of the same class subject to taxation within the territorial limits of the authority levying the tax; and all taxes shall be levied and collected by general laws.
The General Assembly shall have power to divide property into classes and to determine what class or classes of property shall be subject to local taxation. Bonds of the state and of counties, municipalities, taxing and school districts shall not be subject to taxation.

Any law passed or enacted by the General Assembly pursuant to the provisions of or under this amendment, or amended section of the Constitution, classifying property and providing a lower rate of taxation on personal property, tangible or intangible, than upon real estate shall be subject to the referendum power of the people, which is hereby declared to exist to apply only to this section, or amended section. The referendum may be demanded by the people against one or more items, sections, or parts of any act enacted pursuant to or under the power granted by this amendment, or amended section. The referendum petition shall be filed with the Secretary of State not more than four months after the final adjournment of the Legislative Assembly which passed the bill on which the referendum is demanded. The veto power of the Governor shall not extend to measures referred to the people under this section. All elections on measures referred to the people under this act shall be at the regular general election, except when the Legislative Assembly shall order a special election. Any measure referred to the people shall take effect and become a law when approved by the majority of the votes cast thereon, and not otherwise. The whole number of votes cast for the candidates for Governor at the regular election, last preceding the filing of any petition, shall be the basis upon which the legal voters necessary to sign such petition shall be counted. The power of the referendum shall be ordered by the Legislative Assembly at any time any acts or bills are enacted, pursuant to the power granted under this section or amended section, prior to the year of one thousand nine hundred and seventeen. After that time the power of the referendum may be ordered either by the petition signed by five percent of the legal voters or by the Legislative Assembly at the time said acts or bills are enacted. The General Assembly enacting the bill shall provide a way by which the act shall be submitted to the people. The filing of a referendum petition against one or more items, sections or parts of an act, shall not delay the remainder of that act from becoming operative.

Section 172. All property, not exempted from taxation by this Constitution, shall be assessed for taxation at its fair cash value, estimated at the price it would bring at a fair voluntary sale; and any officer, or other person authorized to assess values for taxation, who shall commit any willful error in the performance of his duty, shall be deemed guilty of misfeasance, and upon conviction thereof shall forfeit his office, and be otherwise punished as may be provided by law.

Section 172a. Notwithstanding contrary provisions of Sections 171, 172, or 174 of this Constitution -- The General Assembly shall provide by general law for the assessment for ad valorem tax purposes of agricultural and horticultural land according to the land's value for agricultural or horticultural use. The General Assembly may provide that any change in land use from agricultural or horticultural to another use shall require the levy of an additional tax not to exceed the additional amount that would have been owing had the land been assessed under Section 172 of this Constitution for the current year and the two next preceding years.

The General Assembly may provide for reasonable differences in the rate of ad valorem taxation within different areas of the same taxing districts on that class of property which includes the surface of the land. Those differences shall relate directly to differences between nonrevenue-producing governmental services and benefits giving land urban character which are furnished in one or several areas in contrast to other areas of the taxing district.

Section 172b. Notwithstanding contrary provisions of Sections 170, 171, 172, or 174 of this Constitution, the General Assembly may provide by general law that the governing bodies of county, municipal, and urban-county governments may declare property assessment or reassessment moratoriums for qualifying units of real property for the purpose of encouraging the repair, rehabilitation, or restoration of existing improvements thereon. Prior to the enactment of any property assessment or reassessment moratorium program, the General Assembly shall provide or direct the local governing authority to provide property qualification standards for participation in the program and a limitation on the duration of any assessment or reassessment moratorium. In no instance shall any such moratorium extend beyond five years for any particular unit of real property and improvements thereon.

Section 173. The receiving, directly or indirectly, by any officer of the Commonwealth, or of any county, city or town, or member or officer of the General Assembly, of any interest, profit or perquisites arising from the use or loan of public funds in his hands, or moneys to be raised through his agency for State, city, town, district, or county purposes shall be deemed a felony. Said offense shall be punished as may be prescribed by law, a part of which punishment shall be disqualification to hold office.

Section 174. All property, whether owned by natural persons or corporations, shall be taxed in proportion to its value, unless exempted by this Constitution; and all corporate property shall pay the same rate of taxation paid by individual property. Nothing in this Constitution shall be construed to prevent the General Assembly from providing for taxation based on income, licenses or franchises.

Section 175. The power to tax property shall not be surrendered or suspended by any contract or grant to which the Commonwealth shall be a party.

Section 176. The Commonwealth shall not assume the debt of any county, municipal corporation or political subdivision of the State, unless such debt shall have been contracted to defend itself in time of war, to repel invasion or to suppress insurrection.

Section 177. The credit of the Commonwealth shall not be given, pledged or loaned to any individual, company, corporation or association, municipality, or political subdivision of the State; nor shall the Commonwealth become an owner or stockholder in, nor make donation to, any company, association or corporation; nor shall the Commonwealth construct a railroad or other highway.

Section 178. All laws authorizing the borrowing of money by and on behalf of the Commonwealth, county or other political subdivision of the State, shall specify the purpose for which the money is to be used, and the money so borrowed shall be used for no other purpose.

Section 179. The General Assembly shall not authorize any county or subdivision thereof, city, town or incorporated district, to become a stockholder in any company, association or corporation, or to obtain or appropriate money for, or to loan its credit to, any corporation, association or individual, except for the purpose of constructing or maintaining bridges, turnpike roads, or gravel roads: Provided, If any municipal corporation shall offer to the Commonwealth any property or money for locating or building a Capitol, and the Commonwealth accepts such offer, the corporation may comply with the offer.

Section 180. Every act enacted by the General Assembly, and every ordinance and resolution passed by any county, city, town or municipal board or local legislative body, levying a tax, shall specify distinctly the purpose for which said tax is levied, and no tax levied and collected for one purpose shall ever be devoted to another purpose.

Section 181. The General Assembly shall not impose taxes for the purposes of any county, city, town or other municipal corporation, but may, by general laws, confer on the proper authorities thereof, respectively, the power to assess and collect such taxes. The General Assembly may, by general laws only, provide for the payment of license fees on franchises, stock used for breeding purposes, the various trades, occupations and professions, or a special or excise tax; and may, by general laws, delegate the power to counties, towns, cities and other municipal corporations, to impose and collect license fees on stock used for breeding purposes, on franchises, trades, occupations and professions. And the General Assembly may, by general laws only, authorize cities or towns of any class to provide for taxation for municipal purposes on personal property, tangible and intangible, based on income, licenses or franchises, in lieu of an ad valorem tax thereon: Provided, Cities of the first class shall not be authorized to omit the imposition of an ad valorem tax on such property of any steam railroad, street railway, ferry, bridge, gas, water, heating, telephone, telegraph, electric light or electric power company.

Section 182. Nothing in this Constitution shall be construed to prevent the General Assembly from providing by law how railroads and railroad property shall be assessed and how taxes thereon shall be collected. And until otherwise provided, the present law on said subject shall remain in force.

Education:

Section 183. General Assembly to Provide for School System

The General Assembly shall, by appropriate legislation, provide for an efficient system of common schools throughout the State.

Section 184. Common School Fund -- What Constitutes -- Use -- Vote on Tax for Education other Than in Common Schools

The bond of the Commonwealth issued in favor of the Board of Education for the sum of one million three hundred and twenty-seven thousand dollars shall constitute one bond of the Commonwealth in favor of the Board of Education, and this bond and the seventy-three thousand five hundred dollars of the stock in the Bank of Kentucky, held by the Board of Education, and its proceeds, shall be held inviolate for the purpose of sustaining the system of common schools. The interest and dividends of said fund, together with any sum which may be produced by taxation or otherwise for purposes of common school education, shall be appropriated to the common schools, and to no other purpose. No sum shall be raised or collected for education other than in common schools until the question of taxation is submitted to the legal voters, and the majority of the votes cast at said election shall be in favor of such taxation: Provided, The tax now imposed for educational purposes, and for the endowment and maintenance of the Agricultural and Mechanical College, shall remain until changed by law.

Section 185. Interest on School Fund -- Investment

The General Assembly shall make provision, by law, for the payment of the interest of said school fund, and may provide for the sale of the stock in the Bank of Kentucky; and in case of a sale of all or any part of said stock, the proceeds of sale shall be invested by the Sinking Fund Commissioners in other good interest-bearing stocks or bonds, which shall be subject to sale and reinvestment, from time to time, in like manner, and with the same restrictions, as provided with reference to the sale of the said stock in the Bank of Kentucky.

Section 186. Distribution and Use of School Fund
All funds accruing to the school fund shall be used for the maintenance of the public schools of the Commonwealth, and for no other purpose, and the General Assembly shall by general law prescribe the manner of the distribution of the public school fund among the school districts and its use for public school purposes.

Section 187. Race or Color Not to Affect Distribution of School Fund
In distributing the school fund no distinction shall be made on account of race or color.

Section 188. Refund of Federal Direct Tax Part of School Fund -- Irredeemable Bond
So much of any moneys as may be received by the Commonwealth from the United States under the recent act of Congress refunding the direct tax shall become a part of the school fund, and be held as provided in Section 184; but the General Assembly may authorize the use, by the Commonwealth, of moneys so received or any part thereof, in which event a bond shall be executed to the Board of Education for the amount so used, which bond shall be held on the same terms and conditions, and subject to the provisions of Section 184, concerning the bond therein referred to.

Section 189. School Money Not to Be Used for Church, Sectarian, or Denominational School
No portion of any fund or tax now existing, or that may hereafter be raised or levied for educational purposes, shall be appropriated to, or used by, or in aid of, any church, sectarian or denominational school.

Corporations:

Section 190. Regulation of Corporations by General Assembly

Except as otherwise provided by the Constitution of Kentucky, the General Assembly shall, by general laws only, provide for the formation, organization, and regulation of corporations. Except as otherwise provided by the Constitution of Kentucky, the General Assembly shall also, by general laws only, prescribe the powers, rights, duties, and liabilities of corporations and the powers, rights, duties, and liabilities of their officers and stockholders or members.

Section 191. Repealed.

Section 192. Repealed.

Section 193. Repealed.

Section 194. Repealed.

Section 195. Corporation Property Subject to Eminent Domain -- Corporations Not to Infringe upon Individuals

The Commonwealth, in the exercise of the right of eminent domain, shall have and retain the same powers to take the property and franchises of incorporated companies for public use which it has and retains to take the property of individuals, and the exercise of the police powers of this Commonwealth shall never be abridged nor so construed as to permit corporations to conduct their business in such manner as to infringe upon the equal rights of individuals.

Section 196. Regulation of Common Carriers -- No Relief from Common-Law Liability

Transportation of freight and passengers by railroad, steamboat or other common carrier, shall be so regulated, by general law, as to prevent unjust discrimination. No common carrier shall be permitted to contract for relief from its common law liability.

Section 197. Free Passes or Reduced Rates to Officers Forbidden

No railroad, steamboat or other common carrier, under heavy penalty to be fixed by the General Assembly, shall give a free pass or passes, or shall, at reduced rates not common to the public, sell tickets for transportation to any State, district, city, town or county officer, or member of the General Assembly, or Judge; and any State, district, city, town or county officer, or member of the General Assembly, or Judge, who shall accept or use a free pass or passes, or shall receive or use tickets or transportation at reduced rates not common to the public, shall forfeit his office. It shall be the duty of the General Assembly to enact laws to enforce the provisions of this section.

Section 198. Repealed.

Section 199. Telegraph and Telephone Companies -- Right to Construct Lines -- Exchange of Messages

Any association or corporation, or the lessees or managers thereof, organized for the purpose, or any individual, shall have the right to construct and maintain lines of telegraph within this State, and to connect the same with other lines, and said companies shall receive and transmit each other's messages without unreasonable delay or discrimination, and all such companies are hereby declared to be common carriers and subject to legislative control. Telephone companies operating exchanges in different towns or cities, or other public stations, shall receive and transmit each other's messages without unreasonable delay or discrimination. The General Assembly shall, by general laws of uniform operation, provide reasonable regulations to give full effect to this section. Nothing herein shall be construed to interfere with the rights of cities or towns to arrange and control their streets and alleys, and to designate the places at which, and the manner in which, the wires of such companies shall be erected or laid within the limits of such city or town.

Section 200. Repealed.

Section 201. Public Utility Company Not to Consolidate with, Acquire or Operate Competing or Parallel System -- Common Carriers Not to Share Earnings with One Not Carrying -- Telephone Companies Excepted under Certain Conditions

No railroad, telegraph, telephone, bridge or common carrier company shall consolidate its capital stock, franchises or property, or pool its earnings, in whole or in part, with any other railroad, telegraph, telephone, bridge or common carrier company owning a parallel or competing line or structure, or acquire by purchase, lease or otherwise, any parallel or competing line or structure, or operate the same; nor shall any railroad company or other common carrier combine or make any contract with the owners of any vessel that leaves or makes port in this State, or with any common carrier, by which combination or contract the earnings of one doing the carrying are to be shared by the other not doing the carrying: Provided, however, That telephone companies may acquire by purchase or lease, or otherwise, and operate, parallel or competing exchanges, lines and structures, and the property of other telephone companies, if the state agency as may have jurisdiction over such matters shall first consent thereto, and if, further, each municipality wherein such property or any part thereof is located shall also first consent thereto as to the property within its limits, but under any such acquisition and operation toll line connections with the property so acquired shall be continued and maintained under an agreement between the purchasing company and the toll line companies then furnishing such service, and in the event they are unable to agree as to the terms of such an agreement the state agency as may have jurisdiction over such matters, shall fix the term of such agreement.

Section 202. Repealed.

Section 203. Repealed.

Section 204. Bank Officer Liable for Receiving Deposit for Insolvent Bank

Any President, Director, Manager, Cashier or other officer of any banking institution or association for the deposit or loan of money, or any individual banker, who shall receive or assent to the receiving of deposits after he shall have knowledge of the fact that such banking institution or association or individual banker is insolvent, shall be individually responsible for such deposits so received, and shall be guilty of felony and subject to such punishment as shall be prescribed by law.

Section 205. Forfeiture of Corporate Charters in Case of Abuse or Detrimental Use

The General Assembly shall, by general laws, provide for the revocation or forfeiture of the charters of all corporations guilty of abuse or misuse of their corporate powers, privileges or franchises, or whenever said corporations become detrimental to the interest and welfare of the Commonwealth or its citizens.

Section 206. Warehouses Subject to Legislative Control -- Inspection -- Protection of Patrons

All elevators or storehouses, where grain or other property is stored for a compensation, whether the property stored be kept separate or not, are declared to be public warehouses, subject to legislative control, and the General Assembly shall enact laws for the inspection of grain, tobacco and other produce, and for the protection of producers, shippers and receivers of grain, tobacco and other produce.

Section 207. Repealed.

Section 208. Repealed.

Railroads and Commerce:

Section 209. Repealed.

Section 210. Common Carrier Corporation Not to Be Interested in Other Business

No corporation engaged in the business of common carrier shall, directly or indirectly, own, manage, operate, or engage in any other business than that of a common carrier, or hold, own, lease or acquire, directly or indirectly, mines, factories or timber, except such as shall be necessary to carry on its business, and the General Assembly shall enact laws to give effect to the provisions of this section.

Section 211. Foreign Railroad Corporation May Not Condemn or Acquire Real Estate

No railroad corporation organized under the laws of any other State, or of the United States, and doing business, or proposing to do business, in this State, shall be entitled to the benefit of the right of eminent domain or have power to acquire the right of way or real estate for depot or other uses, until it shall have become a body corporate pursuant to and in accordance with the laws of this Commonwealth.

Section 212. Rolling Stock, Earnings, and Personal Property of Railroads Subject to Execution or Attachment

The rolling stock and other movable property belonging to any railroad corporation or company in this State shall be considered personal property, and shall be liable to execution and sale in the same manner as the personal property of individuals. The earnings of any railroad company or corporation, and choses in action, money and personal property of all kinds belonging to it, in the hands, or under the control, of any officer, agent or employee of such corporation or company, shall be subject to process of attachment to the same extent and in the same manner, as like property of individuals when in the hands or under the control of other persons. Any such earnings, choses in action, money or other personal property may be subjected to the payment of any judgment against such corporation or company, in the same manner and to the same extent as such property of individuals in the hands of third persons.

Section 213. Railroad Companies to Handle Traffic with Connecting Carriers without Discrimination

All railroad, transfer, belt lines and railway bridge companies organized under the laws of Kentucky, or operating, maintaining or controlling any railroad, transfer, belt lines or bridges, or doing a railway business in this State, shall receive, transfer, deliver and switch empty or loaded cars, and shall move, transport, receive, load or unload all the freight in car loads or less quantities, coming to or going from any railroad, transfer, belt line, bridge or siding thereon, with equal promptness and dispatch, and without any discrimination as to charges, preference, drawback or rebate in favor of any person, corporation, consignee or consignor, in any matter as to payment, transportation, handling or delivery; and shall so receive, deliver, transfer and transport all freight as above set forth, from and to any point where there is a physical connection between the tracks of said companies. But this section shall not be construed as requiring any such common carrier to allow the use of its tracks for the trains of another engaged in like business.

Section 214. Railroad Not to Make Exclusive or Preferential Contract

No railway, transfer, belt line or railway bridge company shall make any exclusive or preferential contract or arrangement with any individual, association or corporation, for the receipt, transfer, delivery, transportation, handling, care or custody of any freight, or for the conduct of any business as a common carrier.

Section 215. Freight to Be Handled without Discrimination

All railway, transfer, belt lines or railway bridge companies shall receive, load, unload, transport, haul, deliver and handle freight of the same class for all persons, associations or corporations from and to the same points and upon the same conditions, in the same manner and for the same charges, and for the same method of payment.

Section 216. Railroad Must Allow Tracks of Others to Cross or Unite

All railway, transfer, belt lines and railway bridge companies shall allow the tracks of each other to unite, intersect and cross at any point where such union, intersection and crossing is reasonable or feasible.

Section 217. Penalties for Violating Sections 213, 214, 215, or 216 -- Attorney General to Enforce

Any person, association or corporation, willfully or knowingly violating any of the provisions of Sections 213, 214, 215, or 216, shall, upon conviction by a court of competent jurisdiction, for the first offense be fined two thousand dollars; for the second offense, five thousand dollars; and for the third offense, shall thereupon, ipso facto, forfeit its franchises, privileges or charter rights; and if such delinquent be a foreign corporation, it shall, ipso facto, forfeit its right to do business in this State; and the Attorney-General of the Commonwealth shall forthwith, upon notice of the violation of any of said provisions, institute proceedings to enforce the provisions of the aforesaid sections.

Section 218. Long and Short Hauls

It shall be unlawful for any person or corporation, owning or operating a railroad in this State, or any common carrier, to charge or receive any greater compensation in the aggregate for the transportation of passengers, or of property of like kind, under substantially similar circumstances and conditions, for a shorter than for a longer distance over the same line, in the same direction, the shorter being included within the longer distance; but this shall not be construed as authorizing any common carrier, or person or corporation, owning or operating a railroad in this State, to receive as great compensation for a shorter as for a longer distance: Provided, That upon application to the state agency as may have jurisdiction over such matters, such common carrier, or person or corporation owning or operating a railroad in this State, may in special cases, after investigation by the appropriate state agency, be authorized to charge less for longer than for shorter distances for the transportation of passengers, or property; and the appropriate state agency may, from time to time, prescribe the extent to which such common carrier, or person or corporation, owning or operating a railroad in this State, may be relieved from the operation of this section.

The Militia:

Section 219. Militia, What to Consist of

The militia of the Commonwealth of Kentucky shall consist of all able-bodied male residents of the State between the ages of eighteen and forty-five years, except such persons as may be exempted by the laws of the State or of the United States.

Section 220. General Assembly to Provide for Militia -- Exemptions from Service

The General Assembly shall provide for maintaining an organized militia, and may exempt from military service persons having conscientious scruples against bearing arms; but such persons shall pay an equivalent for such exemption.

Section 221. Government of Militia to Conform to Army Regulations

The organization, equipment and discipline of the militia shall conform as nearly as practicable to the regulations for the government of the armies of the United States.

Section 222. Officers of Militia -- Adjutant General

All militia officers whose appointment is not herein otherwise provided for, shall be elected by persons subject to military duty within their respective companies, battalions, regiments or other commands, under such rules and regulations and for such terms, not exceeding four years, as the General Assembly may, from time to time, direct and establish. The Governor shall appoint an Adjutant-General and his other staff officers; the generals and commandants of regiments and battalions shall respectively appoint their staff officers, and the commandants of companies shall, subject to the approval of their regimental or battalion commanders, appoint their noncommissioned officers. The Governor shall have power to fill vacancies that may occur in elective offices by granting commissions which shall expire when such vacancies have been filled according to the provisions of this Constitution.

Section 223. Safekeeping of Public Arms, Military Records, Relics, and Banners
The General Assembly shall provide for the safekeeping of the public arms, military records, relics and banners of the Commonwealth of Kentucky.

General Provisions:

Section 224. Bonds -- What Officers to Give -- Liability on

The General Assembly shall provide by a general law what officers shall execute bond for the faithful discharge of their duties, and fix the liability therein.

Section 225. Armed Men Not to Be Brought into State -- Exception

No armed person or bodies of men shall be brought into this State for the preservation of the peace or the suppression of domestic violence, except upon the application of the General Assembly, or of the Governor when the General Assembly may not be in session.

Section 226. State Lottery -- Charitable Lotteries and Charitable Gift Enterprises -- Other Lotteries and Gift Enterprises Forbidden

(1) The General Assembly may establish a Kentucky state lottery and may establish a state lottery to be conducted in cooperation with other states. Any lottery so established shall be operated by or on behalf of the Commonwealth of Kentucky.

(2) The General Assembly may by general law permit charitable lotteries and charitable gift enterprises and, if it does so, it shall:

(a) Define what constitutes a charity or charitable organization;

(b) Define the types of charitable lotteries and charitable gift enterprises which may be engaged in;

(c) Set standards for the conduct of charitable lotteries and charitable gift enterprises by charitable organizations;

(d) Provide for means of accounting for the amount of money raised by lotteries and gift enterprises and for assuring its expenditure only for charitable purposes;

(e) Provide suitable penalties for violation of statutes relating to charitable lotteries and charitable gift enterprises; and

(f) Pass whatever other general laws the General Assembly deems necessary to assure the proper functioning, honesty, and integrity of charitable lotteries and charitable gift enterprises, and the charitable purposes for which the funds are expended.

(3) Except as provided in this section, lotteries and gift enterprises are forbidden, and no privileges shall be granted for such purposes, and none shall be exercised, and no schemes for similar purposes shall be allowed. The General Assembly shall enforce this section by proper penalties. All lottery privileges or charters heretofore granted are revoked.

Section 226a. Repealed.

Section 227. Prosecution and Removal of Local Officers for Misfeasance, Malfeasance, or Neglect

Judges of the County Court, Justices of the Peace, Sheriffs, Coroners, Surveyors, Jailers, Assessors, County Attorneys and Constables shall be subject to indictment or prosecution for misfeasance or malfeasance in office, or willful neglect in discharge of official duties, in such mode as may be prescribed by law, and upon conviction his office shall become vacant, but such officer shall have the right to appeal to the Court of Appeals. Provided, also, that the General Assembly may, in addition to the indictment or prosecution above provided, by general law, provide other manner, method or mode for the vacation of office, or the removal from office of any sheriff, jailer, constable or peace officer for neglect of duty, and may provide the method, manner or mode of reinstatement of such officers.

Section 228. Oath of Officers and Attorneys

Members of the General Assembly and all officers, before they enter upon the execution of the duties of their respective offices, and all members of the bar, before they enter upon the practice of their profession, shall take the following oath or affirmation: I do solemnly swear (or affirm, as the case may be) that I will support the Constitution of the United States and the Constitution of this Commonwealth, and be faithful and true to the Commonwealth of Kentucky so long as I continue a citizen thereof, and that I will faithfully execute, to the best of my ability, the office of .... according to law; and I do further solemnly swear (or affirm) that since the adoption of the present Constitution, I, being a citizen of this State, have not fought a duel with deadly weapons within this State nor out of it, nor have I sent or accepted a challenge to fight a duel with deadly weapons, nor have I acted as second in carrying a challenge, nor aided or assisted any person thus offending, so help me God.

Section 229. "Treason" Defined -- Evidence Necessary to Convict
Treason against the Commonwealth shall consist only in levying war against it, or in adhering to its enemies, giving them aid and comfort. No person shall be convicted of treason except on the testimony of two witnesses to the same overt act, or his own confession in open court.

Section 230. Money Not to Be Drawn from Treasury Unless Appropriated -- Annual Publication of Accounts -- Certain Revenues Usable Only for Highway Purposes
No money shall be drawn from the State Treasury, except in pursuance of appropriations made by law; and a regular statement and account of the receipts and expenditures of all public money shall be published annually. No money derived from excise or license taxation relating to gasoline and other motor fuels, and no moneys derived from fees, excise or license taxation relating to registration, operation, or use of vehicles on public highways shall be expended for other than the cost of administration, statutory refunds and adjustments, payment of highway obligations, costs for construction, reconstruction, rights-of-way, maintenance and repair of public highways and bridges, and expense of enforcing state traffic and motor vehicle laws.

Section 231. Suits Against the Commonwealth

The General Assembly may, by law, direct in what manner and in what courts suits may be brought against the Commonwealth.

Section 232. Suits Against the Commonwealth Manner of administering oath.

The manner of administering an oath or affirmation shall be such as is most consistent with the conscience of the deponent, and shall be esteemed by the General Assembly the most solemn appeal to God.

Section 233. General Laws of Virginia in Force in This State until Repealed

All laws which, on the first day of June, one thousand seven hundred and ninety- two, were in force in the State of Virginia, and which are of a general nature and not local to that State, and not repugnant to this Constitution, nor to the laws which have been enacted by the General Assembly of this Commonwealth, shall be in force within this State until they shall be altered or repealed by the General Assembly.

Section 233a. Valid or Recognized Marriage -- Legal Status of Unmarried Individuals

Only a marriage between one man and one woman shall be valid or recognized as a marriage in Kentucky. A legal status identical or substantially similar to that of marriage for unmarried individuals shall not be valid or recognized.

Section 234. Residence and Place of Office of Public Officers

All civil officers for the State at large shall reside within the State, and all district, county, city or town officers shall reside within their respective districts, counties, cities or towns, and shall keep their offices at such places therein as may be required by law.

Section 235. Salaries of Public Officers Not to Be Changed During Term -- Deductions for Neglect

The salaries of public officers shall not be changed during the terms for which they were elected; but it shall be the duty of the General Assembly to regulate, by a general law, in what cases and what deductions shall be made for neglect of official duties. This section shall apply to members of the General Assembly also.

Section 236. When Officers to Enter upon Duties

The General Assembly shall, by law, prescribe the time when the several officers authorized or directed by this Constitution to be elected or appointed, shall enter upon the duties of their respective offices, except where the time is fixed by this Constitution.

Section 237. Federal Office Incompatible with State Office

No member of Congress, or person holding or exercising an office of trust or profit under the United States, or any of them, or under any foreign power, shall be eligible to hold or exercise any office of trust or profit under this Constitution, or the laws made in pursuance thereof.

Section 238. Discharge of Sureties on Officers' Bonds

The General Assembly shall direct by law how persons who now are, or may hereafter become, sureties for public officers, may be relieved of or discharged from suretyship.

Section 239. Disqualification from Office for Presenting or Accepting Challenge to Duel -- Further Punishment

Any person who shall, after the adoption of this Constitution, either directly or indirectly, give, accept or knowingly carry a challenge to any person or persons to fight in single combat, with a citizen of this State, with a deadly weapon, either in or out of the State, shall be deprived of the right to hold any office of honor or profit in this Commonwealth; and if said acts, or any of them, be committed within this State, the person or persons so committing them shall be further punished in such manner as the General Assembly may prescribe by law.

Section 240. Pardon of Person Convicted of Dueling
The Governor shall have power, after five years from the time of the offense, to pardon any person who shall have participated in a duel as principal, second or otherwise, and to restore him to all the rights, privileges and immunities to which he was entitled before such participation. Upon presentation of such pardon the oath prescribed in Section 228 shall be varied to suit the case.

Section 241. Recovery for Wrongful Death
Whenever the death of a person shall result from an injury inflicted by negligence or wrongful act, then, in every such case, damages may be recovered for such death, from the corporations and persons so causing the same. Until otherwise provided by law, the action to recover such damages shall in all cases be prosecuted by the personal representative of the deceased person. The General Assembly may provide how the recovery shall go and to whom belong; and until such provision is made, the same shall form part of the personal estate of the deceased person.

Section 242. Just Compensation to Be Made in Condemning Private Property -- Right of Appeal -- Jury Trial
Municipal and other corporations, and individuals invested with the privilege of taking private property for public use, shall make just compensation for property taken, injured or destroyed by them; which compensation shall be paid before such taking, or paid or secured, at the election of such corporation or individual, before such injury or destruction. The General Assembly shall not deprive any person of an appeal from any preliminary assessment of damages against any such corporation or individual made by Commissioners or otherwise; and upon appeal from such preliminary assessment, the amount of such damages shall, in all cases, be determined by a jury, according to the course of the common law.

Section 243. Child Labor

The General Assembly shall, by law, fix the minimum ages at which children may be employed in places dangerous to life or health, or injurious to morals; and shall provide adequate penalties for violations of such law.

Section 244. Wage-earners in Industry or of Corporations to Be Paid in Money

All wage-earners in this State employed in factories, mines, workshops, or by corporations, shall be paid for their labor in lawful money. The General Assembly shall prescribe adequate penalties for violations of this section.

Section 244a. Old Age Assistance

The General Assembly shall prescribe such laws as may be necessary for the granting and paying of old persons an annuity or pension.

Section 245. Revision of Statutes to Conform to Constitution

Upon the promulgation of this Constitution, the Governor shall appoint three persons, learned in the law, who shall be Commissioners to revise the statute laws of this Commonwealth, and prepare amendments thereto, to the end that the statute laws shall conform to and effectuate this Constitution. Such revision and amendments shall be laid before the next General Assembly for adoption or rejection, in whole or in part. The said Commissioners shall be allowed ten dollars each per day for their services, and also necessary stationery for the time during which they are actually employed; and upon their certificate the Auditor shall draw his warrant upon the Treasurer. They shall have the power to employ clerical assistants, at a compensation not exceeding ten dollars per day in the aggregate. If the Commissioners, or any of them, shall refuse to act, or a vacancy shall occur, the Governor shall appoint another or others in his or their place.

Section 246. Maximum Limit on Compensation of Public Officers

No public officer or employee except the Governor, shall receive as compensation per annum for official services, exclusive of the compensation of legally authorized deputies and assistants which shall be fixed and provided for by law, but inclusive of allowance for living expenses, if any, as may be fixed and provided for by law, any amount in excess of the following sums: Officers whose jurisdiction or duties are coextensive with the Commonwealth, the mayor of any city of the first class, and Judges and Commissioners of the Court of Appeals, Twelve Thousand Dollars ($12,000); Circuit Judges, Eight Thousand Four Hundred Dollars ($8,400); all other public officers, Seven Thousand Two Hundred Dollars ($7,200). Compensation within the limits of this amendment may be authorized by the General Assembly to be paid, but not retroactively, to public officers in office at the time of its adoption, or who are elected at the election at which this amendment is adopted. Nothing in this amendment shall permit any officer to receive, for the year 1949, any compensation in excess of the limit in force prior to the adoption of this amendment.

Section 247. Public Printing -- Contract for -- Officers Not to Have Interest in -- Governor to Approve

The printing and binding of the laws, journals, department reports, and all other public printing and binding, shall be performed under contract, to be given to the lowest responsible bidder, below such maximum and under such regulations as may be prescribed by law. No member of the General Assembly, or officer of the Commonwealth, shall be in any way interested in any such contract; and all such contracts shall be subject to the approval of the Governor.

Section 248. Juries -- Number of Jurors -- Three-fourths May Indict or Give Verdict

A grand jury shall consist of twelve persons, nine of whom concurring, may find an indictment. In civil and misdemeanor cases, in courts inferior to the Circuit Courts, a jury shall consist of six persons. The General Assembly may provide that in any or all trials of civil actions in the Circuit Courts, three-fourths or more of the jurors concurring may return a verdict, which shall have the same force and effect as if rendered by the entire panel. But where a verdict is rendered by a less number than the whole jury, it shall be signed by all the jurors who agree to it.

Section 249. Employees of General Assembly -- Number and Compensation

The House of Representatives of the General Assembly shall not elect, appoint, employ or pay for, exceeding one Chief Clerk, one Assistant Clerk, one Enrolling Clerk, one Sergeant at Arms, one Doorkeeper, one Janitor, two Cloakroom Keepers and four Pages; and the Senate shall not elect, appoint, employ or pay for, exceeding one Chief Clerk, one Assistant Clerk, one Enrolling Clerk, one Sergeant at Arms, one Doorkeeper, one Janitor, one Cloakroom Keeper and three Pages; and the General Assembly shall provide, by general law, for fixing the per diem or salary of all of said employees.

Section 250. Arbitration, Method for to Be Provided

It shall be the duty of the General Assembly to enact such laws as shall be necessary and proper to decide differences by arbitrators, the arbitrators to be appointed by the parties who may choose that summary mode of adjustment.

Section 251. Limitation of Actions to Recover Possession of Land Based on Early Patents

No action shall be maintained for possession of any lands lying within this State, where it is necessary for the claimant to rely for his recovery on any grant or patent issued by the Commonwealth of Virginia, or by the Commonwealth of Kentucky prior to the year one thousand eight hundred and twenty, against any person claiming such lands by possession to a well-defined boundary, under a title of record, unless such action shall be instituted within five years after this Constitution shall go into effect, or within five years after the occupant may take possession; but nothing herein shall be construed to affect any right, title or interest in lands acquired by virtue of adverse possession under the laws of this Commonwealth.

Section 252. Houses of Reform to Be Established and Maintained

It shall be the duty of the General Assembly to provide by law, as soon as practicable, for the establishment and maintenance of an institution or institutions for the detention, correction, instruction and reformation of all persons under the age of eighteen years, convicted of such felonies and such misdemeanors as may be designated by law. Said institution shall be known as the "House of Reform."[

Section 253. Working of Penitentiary Prisoners -- When and Where Permitted

Persons convicted of felony and sentenced to confinement in the penitentiary shall be confined at labor within the walls of the penitentiary; and the General Assembly shall not have the power to authorize employment of convicts elsewhere, except upon the public works of the Commonwealth of Kentucky, or when, during pestilence or in case of the destruction of the prison buildings, they cannot be confined in the penitentiary.

That Section 253 of the Constitution be amended so that the Commonwealth of Kentucky may use and employ outside of the walls of the penitentiaries in such manner and means as may be provided by law, persons convicted of felony and sentenced to confinement in the penitentiary for the purpose of constructing or reconstructing and maintaining public roads and public bridges or for the purpose of making and preparing material for public roads and bridges, and that the Commonwealth of Kentucky may, by the use and employment of convict labor outside of the walls of the penitentiary by other ways or means, as may be provided by law, aid the counties for road and bridge purposes, work on the State farm or farms.

Section 254. Control and Support of Convicts -- Leasing of Labor
The Commonwealth shall maintain control of the discipline, and provide for all supplies, and for the sanitary condition of the convicts, and the labor only of convicts may be leased.

Section 255. Frankfort is State Capital
The seat of government shall continue in the city of Frankfort, unless removed by a vote of two-thirds of each House of the first General Assembly which convenes after the adoption of this Constitution.

Section 255a. Personal right to hunt, fish, and harvest wildlife - Limitations.
The citizens of Kentucky have the personal right to hunt, fish, and harvest wildlife, using traditional methods, subject only to statutes enacted by the Legislature, and to administrative regulations adopted by the designated state agency to promote wildlife conservation and management and to preserve the future of hunting and fishing. Public hunting and fishing shall be a preferred means of managing and controlling wildlife. This section shall not be construed to modify any provision of law relating to trespass, property rights, or the regulation of commercial activities.

Mode of Revision:

Section 256. Amendments to Constitution -- How proposed and voted upon.

Amendments to this Constitution may be proposed in either House of the General Assembly at a regular session, and if such amendment or amendments shall be agreed to by three-fifths of all the members elected to each House, such proposed amendment or amendments, with the yeas and nays of the members of each House taken thereon, shall be entered in full in their respective journals. Then such proposed amendment or amendments shall be submitted to the voters of the State for their ratification or rejection at the next general election for members of the House of Representatives, the vote to be taken thereon in such manner as the General Assembly may provide, and to be certified by the officers of election to the Secretary of State in such manner as shall be provided by law, which vote shall be compared and certified by the same board authorized by law to compare the polls and give certificates of election to officers for the State at large. If it shall appear that a majority of the votes cast for and against an amendment at said election was for the amendment, then the same shall become a part of the Constitution of this Commonwealth, and shall be so proclaimed by the Governor, and published in such manner as the General Assembly may direct. Said amendments shall not be submitted at an election which occurs less than ninety days from the final passage of such proposed amendment or amendments. Not more than four amendments shall be voted upon at any one time. If two or more amendments shall be submitted at the same time, they shall be submitted in such manner that the electors shall vote for or against each of such amendments separately, but an amendment may relate to a single subject or to related subject matters and may amend or modify as many articles and as many sections of the Constitution as may be necessary and appropriate in order to accomplish the objectives of the amendment. The approval of the Governor shall not be necessary to any bill, order, resolution or vote of the General Assembly, proposing an amendment or amendments to this

Constitution.

Section 257. Publication of proposed amendments.
Before an amendment shall be submitted to a vote, the Secretary of State shall cause such proposed amendment, and the time that the same is to be voted upon, to be published at least ninety days before the vote is to be taken thereon in such manner as may be prescribed by law.

Section 258. Constitutional Convention -- How proposed, voted upon, and called.
When a majority of all the members elected to each House of the General Assembly shall concur, by a yea and nay vote, to be entered upon their respective journals, in enacting a law to take the sense of the people of the State as to the necessity and expediency of calling a Convention for the purpose of revising or amending this Constitution, and such amendments as may have been made to the same, such law shall be spread upon their respective journals. If the next General Assembly shall, in like manner, concur in such law, it shall provide for having a poll opened in each voting precinct in this state by the officers provided by law for holding general elections at the next ensuing regular election to be held for State officers or members of the House of Representatives, which does not occur within ninety days from the final passage of such law, at which time and places the votes of the qualified voters shall be taken for and against calling the Convention, in the same manner provided by law for taking votes in other State elections. The vote for and against said proposition shall be certified to the Secretary of State by the same officers and in the same manner as in State elections. If it shall appear that a majority voting on the proposition was for calling a Convention, and if the total number of votes cast for the calling of the Convention is equal to one-fourth of the number of qualified voters who voted at the last preceding general election in this State, the Secretary of State shall certify the same to the General Assembly at its next regular session, at which session a law shall be enacted calling a Convention to readopt, revise or amend this Constitution, and

such amendments as may have been made thereto.

Section 259. Number and qualifications of delegates
The Convention shall consist of as many delegates as there are members of the House of Representatives; and the delegates shall have the same qualifications and be elected from the same districts as said Representatives.

Section 260. Election of delegates -- meeting.
Delegates to such Convention shall be elected at the next general State election after the passage of the act calling the Convention, which does not occur within less than ninety days; and they shall meet within ninety days after their election at the Capital of the State, and continue in session until their work is completed.

Section 261. Certification of election and compensation of delegates.
The General Assembly, in the act calling the Convention, shall provide for comparing the polls and giving certificates of election to the delegates elected, and provide for their compensation.

Section 262. Determination of election and qualifications of delegates -- Contests.
The Convention, when assembled, shall be the judge of the election and qualification of its members, and shall determine contested elections. But the General Assembly shall, in the act calling the Convention, provide for taking testimony in such cases, and for issuing a writ of election in case of a tie.

Section 263. Notice of election on question of calling convention.
Before a vote is taken upon the question of calling a Convention, the Secretary of State shall cause notice of the election to be published in such manner as may be provided by the act directing said vote to be taken.

Schedule and Ordinance

Schedule:

That no inconvenience may arise from the alterations and amendments made in this Constitution, and in order to carry the same into complete operation, it is hereby declared and ordained:

First: That all laws of this Commonwealth in force at the time of the adoption of this Constitution, not inconsistent therewith, shall remain in full force until altered or repealed by the General Assembly; and all rights, actions, prosecutions, claims and contracts of the State, counties, individuals or bodies corporate, not inconsistent therewith, shall continue as valid as if this Constitution had not been adopted. The provisions of all laws which are inconsistent with this Constitution shall cease upon its adoption, except that all laws which are inconsistent with such provisions as require legislation to enforce them shall remain in force until such legislation is had, but not longer than six years after the adoption of this Constitution, unless sooner amended or repealed by the General Assembly.

Second: That all recognizances, obligations and all other instruments entered into or executed before the adoption of this Constitution, to the State, or to any city, town, county or subdivision thereof, and all fines, taxes, penalties and forfeitures due or owing to this State, or to any city, town, county or subdivision thereof; and all writs, prosecutions, actions and causes of action, except as otherwise herein provided, shall continue and remain unaffected by the adoption of this Constitution. And all indictments which shall have been found, or may hereafter be found, for any crime or offense committed before this Constitution takes effect, may be prosecuted as if no change had taken place, except as otherwise provided in this Constitution.

Third: All Circuit, Chancery, Criminal, Law and Equity, Law, and Common Pleas Courts, as now constituted and organized by law, shall continue with their respective jurisdictions until the Judges of the Circuit Courts provided for in this Constitution shall have been elected and qualified, and shall then cease and determine; and the causes, actions and proceedings then pending in said first named courts, which are discontinued by this Constitution, shall be transferred to, and tried by, the Circuit Courts in the counties, respectively, in which said causes, actions and proceedings are pending.

Fourth: The Treasurer, Attorney-General, Auditor of Public Accounts, Superintendent of Public Instruction, and Register of the Land Office, elected in eighteen hundred and ninety-one, shall hold their offices until the first Monday in January, eighteen hundred and ninety-six, and until the election and qualification of their successors. The Governor and Lieutenant Governor elected in eighteen hundred and ninety-one shall hold their offices until the sixth Tuesday after the first Monday in November, eighteen hundred and ninety-five, and until their successors are elected and qualified. The Governor and Treasurer elected in eighteen hundred and ninety-one shall be ineligible to the succeeding term. The Governor elected in eighteen hundred and ninety-one may appoint a Secretary of State and a Commissioner of Agriculture, Labor and Statistics, as now provided, who shall hold their offices until their successors are elected and qualified, unless sooner removed by the Governor. The official bond of the present Treasurer shall be renewed at the expiration of two years from the time of his qualification.

Fifth: All officers who may be in office at the adoption of this Constitution, or who may be elected before the election of their successors, as provided in this Constitution, shall hold their respective offices until their successors are elected or appointed and qualified as provided in this Constitution.

Sixth: The Quarterly Courts created by this Constitution shall be the successors of the present statutory Quarterly Courts in the several counties of this State; and all suits, proceedings, prosecutions, records and judgments now pending or being in said last named courts shall, after the adoption of this Constitution, be transferred to the Quarterly Courts created by this Constitution, and shall proceed as though the same had been therein instituted

Ordinance

We, the representatives of the people of Kentucky, in Convention assembled, in their name and by their authority and in virtue of the power vested in us as Delegates from the counties and districts respectively affixed to our names, do ordain and proclaim the foregoing to be the Constitution of the Commonwealth of Kentucky from and after this date.
Done at Frankfort this twenty-eighth day of September, in the year of our Lord one thousand eight hundred and ninety-one, and in the one hundredth year of the Commonwealth.

www.ingramcontent.com/pod-product-compliance
Lightning Source LLC
Chambersburg PA
CBHW070150230526
45471CB00002B/599